SANDBOX PERSONALITIES

WHEN GROWN-UPS BEHAVE LIKE TODDLERS PLAYING IN A SANDBOX

ALLEN FORBES

www.AFspeaks.com

SANDBOX PERSONALITIES
Copyright © 2016 by Allen Forbes
ISBN-10: 0997712309
ISBN-13: 978-0-9977123-0-8

Printed in the United States of America. All rights reserved under international copyright law. Contents and/or cover may not be reproduced in whole or part without the express written consent of the publisher.

Published by Allen Forbes
P.O. Box 305
Germantown, MD 20875

Library of Congress Control Number: 2016911004

Cover design by Tracy Jackson
Media Cyctems

Knowing who is
in the Sandbox with you
can make all of the difference

Table of Contents

Acknowledgements..1
Introduction...3
Chapter 1 The Taker..5
Chapter 2 The Eater..19
Chapter 3 The Crusher-Hater....................................31
Chapter 4 The Pooper..43
Chapter 5 The Thrower..55
Chapter 6 The Complainer..67
Chapter 7 The My-Sander...79
Chapter 8 The Share-Sander......................................91
Chapter 9 Driving Factors..109
Chapter 10 Moving Forward.....................................125
Personalities/Traits Quick Guide.....................................132
References...134
About the Author...135

Acknowledgements

This project has taken me many years to complete and I could have never completed it on my own. There have been countless individuals who both knowingly and unknowingly assisted me. With that being said, I would specifically like to acknowledge the following individuals for their assistance and talent: Jeannie Waldren, Dr. McCray, Ramona Turner, Connie Howard, Sabrina Murray, Bobbette Gordon and Jean Williams – thank you for your time. Your feedback, advice, editing and overall contributions were crucial to this project. Many thanks and appreciation to Tracy Jackson www.mediacyctems.tv , for his creativity with the book cover design.

I would also like to give my gratitude to my lovely wife, Lloyda, who has supported me and encouraged me since we have been married. You have helped me in such a great way and I would like to let you know how much I really appreciate you, and the precious gift that you are in my life.

I would like to thank all of you for helping to make my sandbox experience a good one!

Introduction

Sandbox Personalities discusses the behaviors that toddlers exhibit when they are put in the sandbox to play. The Sandbox represents life and the sand represents what we build in life. The Sandbox is that place where we build our lives, and ultimately our future. It also represents the place where our relationships occur. As you will see, not much has changed between adulthood and childhood, as it pertains to our behavior in the sandbox or how we relate to each other. As adults, we sometimes behave like toddlers playing in a sandbox. The children in the sandbox are the adults that we have become; without letting go of the childish behavior. There are Takers, Crushers/Haters, Eaters, Complainers, My Sanders, Sharers, Throwers, and yes, even Poopers in the Sandbox.

When grown-ups behave like toddlers playing in a sandbox, things can become crazy and unnerving. Why do they act like this? What causes this behavior? How do we deal with them? All of these are valid questions and the answers can be found in this book - Sandbox Personalities.

The fact is, many adults *have kept the personalities and behaviors that they exhibited as young children!* So, although they are 'grown-ups,' the behaviors that they exhibit when they are faced with certain people, situations and circumstances are really not very 'grown up' at all. They tend to behave in certain childish ways when their needs are not met, or when they are faced with stress and disappointments. For many of us, the toddler inside still manages to show up with his/her behavior during difficult times.

The purpose of this book is to encourage and assist you to move toward congruent relationships through a better understanding of yourself and those around you, by maximizing strengths and navigating challenging behaviors. This book will highlight *some* of the driving factors behind the behaviors; the strengths and the challenges, and what can be done to make any 'grown-up' changes. While some of the driving factors are the same for different personalities, you will find that the exhibited behavior is different because of the individual's "lens" – which is how they see things and internalize people and situations. Don't worry; in the process you'll gain some techniques that you can use to have better relationships with those you live, work, and interact with.

Join me as we take a closer look at the "Sandbox," and the behavior of some of the individuals, as they come to play and build in the sand.

Knowing who is in the Sandbox with you can make all of the difference

Chapter One

The Taker

When self-control is absent, you will always find addictive behaviors present.

"Take your Sand" Personality
Napoleon / Hitler complex
"The Taking Relationship"

It's Tuesday morning and 4-year old Harry is going to the park with his Dad to play in the sandbox. He and his Dad have just moved to the neighborhood and they are still discovering the area. Tired of unpacking, dad decides to take him to the park to meet other parents and their kids, so that both he and Harry could make new friends. Dad puts Harry into the sandbox with two other toddlers – Karen and Jimmy – while he chats with their parents. Karen and Jimmy are playing on opposite sides of the sandbox with their miniature shovels and buckets, building sandcastles. Harry, new to the sandbox, begins playing with his shovel and bucket as well.

Not long after being in the sandbox, Harry sees that Karen's shovel is different from his. He decides that he wants it. So he reaches over and takes her shovel. Harry then decides that he wants Karen's bucket also, because he thinks that having the bucket and the shovel will make things easier for him to build his castle. However, not only does he take her bucket but he decides to take the sand that is on her side of the sandbox, as well. In spite of Karen's tears and distress, Harry moved the sand from Karen's side of the sandbox over to his area to begin building his bigger and/or better sandcastle. Harry is not happy with what he has, and instead he wants more. He believes that more will make him happy and that he deserves to have what he wants when he wants it. He does not take into consideration anyone else in his quest for more, nor does he care about how others feel as a result of his actions.

Harry's interactions are much like the story of a [2]king and the farmer who owned some land near the palace, which he developed and cultivated and turned into a vineyard. One day, from the palace window, the king looked over at the farmer's vineyard and he really admired the vineyard and the crop that it produced. So, the king went over to talk with the farmer to see if he would trade or sell his land. The farmer replied that this was his family's inheritance and there was no way that he would sell or trade something that meant so much to him and his family.

The king was very upset by the farmer's reply. He went to his bedroom, laid down on his bed and became deeply depressed. Not only was he depressed, but he became so obsessed with the desire to own the farmer's vineyard that he refused to eat. The queen came to see the King after the servants told her of his depression. After he told her that the farmer would not sell or trade his vineyard, the queen told the king to get up and eat something and that she would make sure that the he got the vineyard that he desired. The queen then sent to the elders of the city and said, "Have the farmer report to the palace and then have two false witnesses come forward and say that the farmer has cursed God and the king. After he is found guilty, kill this farmer and all of his children. Let me know when this is done."

The elders did as they were directed and notified the queen when the dirty deeds were done. The queen then told the king to go and **take** possession of the vineyard that once belonged to the farmer. Although it was the queen, and not the king who did the conniving to steal this vineyard, they are both categorized as Takers of a property that was not rightfully theirs. The Taker always wants to benefit from someone else's hard work. Instead of giving the necessary time to cultivate and then reap a harvest, Takers look for an immediate harvest. So, upon seeing things that are already developed by others, they just take what they see without the care or feelings of another. As we learn from the story of the king and the farmer, Takers also become depressed when they do not get what they want. The longer they go without their desires being met, the more obsessed they become, to the point of neglecting themselves.

The Taker is on a quest to obtain more. Takers also do not feel badly about taking what does not belong to them. A Taker's reasoning says that taking from you does not make them a bad person, just someone who knows what they want and is not afraid to go get it. There always seems to be a justification for taking what is not theirs. Takers make excuses for their behavior so that they do not feel condemned about their actions. In the case of the king, his rationale was that the vineyard was near to the palace and that reason was enough. The queen's rationale was that because they were in a position of authority they should have whatever they wanted. This mindset gives the Takers the ability to justify their negative behavior.

- Greed, Bullying, Stinginess, Pride

Takers have learned to apply the trait of persistence; if they don't quit, they can end up having what they desire. Unfortunately, because they are so focused on what is in front of them, Takers often do not see the trouble that they cause others as they pursue their desires. Takers believe that they can do whatever it takes to have what they want. They will run you over to get it. In some cases, because this behavior often works for them, they begin to care less about the hurt people in their path. There is an unbalanced desire (greed) to have more. Sharing is not an option.

This thinking and behavior is established on the foundation of pride. Pride produces self-centeredness. When people are prideful, they think about themselves first; their importance, their needs, and their desires. They know that others are around them, but they cannot really see them because they are too focused on themselves. The problem with looking at yourself (your importance, needs and desires) is that you do not see a complete picture. While Takers may accomplish great things and have great accumulations of things, they often miss out on the true riches in life. When greed, bullying and pride are the basis for behavior, a portion of peace is lost. How does it profit them to lose their soul and peace by the acquisition of things?

- Working and relating with others is challenging

Takers of the sand don't usually like to work with others. However, there are times when they will join with others who are like-minded to accomplish a specific goal. If they do work with other Takers, there will be some type of hierarchy and whoever is strongest will be submitted to. Everyone around a Taker is sized up in this fashion – "Do I submit to you, or do you submit to me?" They are constantly sizing up other individuals who they work with and who are around them. Therefore, it is interesting to note that when they feel weaker around other Takers, they will take a subordinate role.

When a Taker is looking for a relationship, he/she is looking for a person who they can dominate. The accumulation of things is evidence of control to a Taker, and that control; whether it is material, or a personal relationship – is important. The Taker's mindset is: "control equals power." Takers love to take control in their relationships. However, their aim is not necessarily to make the other person weak, the aim is to maintain their dominant position.

Unfortunately, a Taker will often view those who do not have control as weak and not worthy of respect. Therefore, when working with or having interactions with others, the ideas and contributions of 'weaker folks" are not acknowledged. A Taker has a difficult time listening to someone they view as being weaker than them. If they were to listen to someone weaker than they are, that would make them seem weak. They don't see what value a "weaker" person can bring to the equation. This mindset is often a limiting factor to growth in business, personal relationships and intimacy in a marriage.

- "Everybody owes me"

A common mindset for a Taker is "everybody owes me…including God." Takers see no problem with using you, your things, or eating your food because they wanted it. After all, they believe they are entitled to what they want even if you own it. Sometimes you may be an afterthought, once they have taken what they want. The thought of you or your feelings is quickly dismissed by the next selfish thought that they have. It is extremely difficult for a Taker to see that they are doing anything wrong. To them, all of their actions are justified.

- Following established laws or rules (authority) is hard

A Taker chooses not to follow established laws and boundaries if they stand in the way of them getting what they want. Laws and authority will only be followed if they can achieve what they desire. This means that all Takers are law-breakers. To take something that does not belong to you breaks the *universal* law of love, not to mention legal laws. As stated previously, the Taker only respects power and not just authority. Let me explain:

The Taker can be in the marketplace and have a boss whom they don't respect because that person is seen as weak to them. Takers will often use intimidation to influence the interaction that they have with their boss because they don't respect his/her authority. They may follow the boss' direction when they are around, but once the boss is gone, they do what they want, because they don't respect the boss, or their authority. On the other hand, the Taker who has a boss who is seen as being powerful and having authority: will respect and follow that individual. This goes along with the hierarchical thinking and 'sizing up' of those who are around them. Takers believe that they make the rules and they set up the boundaries for others to follow. The rules and boundaries change based on what they want and/or need at the time.

- Lacking self-control, easily angered and hostile

Takers are usually very fragile individuals, but you would never be able to tell that from looking at their outward appearance (external landscape.) While they are really after external control, they themselves lack self-control. *Self-control is a defense mechanism.* It allows us to protect ourselves. By exerting self-control we can bring balance and even put an end to any behavior that is not to our advantage. Takers lack restraint because they-want-what-they-want-when-they-want-it. This lack of restraint causes

Takers to be easily angered and become hostile and raging, often over little things.

[1]Self-control is *control, or restraint of oneself or one's thoughts, actions and feelings.* Because self-control is a defense system within a person's soul, it is easily susceptible to contamination. In the same manner, if the physical defenses were broken down in the body, then one would become susceptible to physical diseases or contamination. So, when spiritual defenses like self-control are broken down in the soul, one can contract spiritual contaminants such as addiction, anger, hostility, rage, strife, hatred, and unforgiveness…to name a few. Someone who flows with this type of negative energy will begin to attract negative things to their life as a result.

Self-control is what causes the internal defense system to work the right way; prohibiting negative things from taking root in the soul and growing. Once something negative is planted in the seat of the soul (internally) it will eventually become evident (externally) to all. It is ironic that most Takers struggle with addictive behaviors because having control is a driving force for a Taker. However, they usually end up being controlled by addictions, and therefore are not in control at all. The word [1]*addiction* means being enslaved to a habit or practice psychologically or physically. Its origin comes from a Latin word that means "*a giving-over, or surrender.*" **When self-control is absent, you will always find addictions (particularly behavior) present.**

- Self-worth is found in material and psychological possessions

A Taker's self-worth comes from a feeling of control, which comes from what they possess. One of the reasons that a Taker is addicted to *take-ing* is that *take-ing* gives that feeling of power and control. Control equals security. When they feel less adequate than others, they try to find security through dominating others and in the things that they possess. Takers are insecure individuals. Self-confidence is absent. So, the strong and confident exterior they portray is usually just a facade. There is something deep down on the inside that makes them feel inferior, and triggers the behavior that makes them want to be superior. The Taker forms an artificial barrier in an attempt to cover their very weaknesses. A Taker usually has an absence of <u>self-control</u>, <u>self-worth</u>, <u>self-confidence</u> and <u>security</u> (the 4-Ss.)

> [1]**Self-control**: Control or restraint of oneself or one's actions and feelings.
>
> [1]**Self-Worth**: The sense of one's own value or worth as a person; self-esteem. Self-respect.
>
> [1]**Self Confidence**: Realistic confidence in one's own judgment, powers, ability, etc.
>
> My definition follows: Freedom from doubt; belief in yourself and your abilities.
>
> [1]**Security**: Something that secures or makes safe; protection; defense.

- Fear of not having enough, or losing what they have

Fear is a terrible taskmaster. The biggest fear for a Taker is losing what he has accumulated in material and psychological possessions. His thinking is that all self-worth, confidence, and security are in what is accumulated. The problem with this thinking is that everything that we can see is temporary. We were never created to get our self-worth, confidence and security from things or from other people. Because a Taker does not truly understand who he/she really is and what are the true riches in life, Takers will look to material things to satisfy their quest for true identity. Therefore, when things and status change, so does the Taker's self-worth, confidence and security. An individual's overall worth should be measured based on their internal content and not just what they hold in their hands. What really creates a positive, powerful individual is integrity, kindness, responsibility, and character. These are the things that can't be taken from someone who really possesses them.

[2]There once was a Landlord who owned a vineyard that he leased to some business associates. He went away to his homeland for an extended period of time. Before he left, he left them with the understanding that they could cultivate the vineyard but they needed to give him a share of the profits each year. When the time for harvest came, he sent his Assistant to go to the business associates and get his share of the profits. Because the business associates had a "Taker" mentality, they immediately became hostile and beat the Assistant, and sent him away empty-handed. The same thing happens quite a few more times, as the Landlord continues to send other Assistants to get what is due him. Still seeing the same results, he decided that he would send his only son assuming that the business

associates would show respect toward him. However, the Takers plotted among themselves to kill the son because he was the heir, and then keep all of the profits for themselves.

A common attitude of Takers is revealed in the story above. They are obsessed with accumulating and they don't care who gets hurt in the process. Also, it is important to note that the business associates (Takers) are working together as a team because they are all like-minded. They have little regard for the owner, or his authority. He's not there and he's considered weak. They believe that they are entitled to have "what they want when they want it". After justifying their actions, they easily take from others what is not rightfully theirs without having any guilt.

- Blaming others

Takers are also full of excuses and want to blame others, when they should take responsibility; they also have a tendency to display destructive behaviors and will blame others for their own actions. You might hear a Taker say, "they made me do that, because…" or, "if you would have done this, then I wouldn't have done that." This is another aspect of lacking self-control. Takers really believe that their behavior is the result of someone else's actions. They have learned how to live a reactionary life. [A person who reacts is always predictable because they have a habit of doing the same thing when presented with a particular situation or circumstance.] Being a creature of habit, makes a Taker reactionary, instead of one who thinks, considers and then acts (a responder.) With a Taker on your team, or in a relationship, beware that they will often not own up to responsibility and will blame everyone else -- and possibly you --when things don't end up the way they expected.

- Having a relationship with a Taker

Being in a relationship with a Taker can be trying. From the Taker's perspective, he or she is in the relationship to receive (not to give) and usually, when a Taker gives, it is only to receive something in return. Whenever the Taker gives, they are ready to receive almost immediately. If, after giving something, they do not receive what they want, an argument or fight will usually break out soon after. A relationship between two Takers is often very volatile and can include physical altercations. Since both of them are concentrating on their own needs, neither person in the relationship is fulfilled. Focusing more on your own needs than the needs of the person you are in a relationship with is unbalanced, or lopsided. This lopsidedness seems normal to a Taker. As a result, the intimacy or harmony in this relationship is little to none, and remains that way until someone in the relationship is willing to change. In any good relationship, the focus has to be on meeting each other's needs. If not, there will be a lot of fighting and struggling going on in that relationship. Takers don't look at things from the other individual's point of view because they can only see their own goals, needs and desires. Even when a Taker gives, they give much less than they would like to receive.

Someone in a relationship with a Taker has to be a very giving and sharing person, in order for the relationship to work. In most relationships between well-meaning, mature people, your habits will usually rub off on each other. This can be a plus, and sometimes a negative.

Strengths and Challenges of a Taker Personality

Strengths: Focus, Determination, Natural Leadership, Strong will.

Challenges: Lack of self-control, Anger, Hostility, Blaming others when things go wrong, Addictive behaviors, Misplaced self-worth, and an Inflated self-confidence.

Chapter Two

The Eater

The things that we fight with internally, and lose to, will always show up externally in our behaviors.

"Eat the Sand" Personality

Claire pushes the stroller with Robert, her son, into the playground area and says hello to a few friends, then she heads toward the sandbox where she will let Robert play. She normally stays with Robert and they play together in the sandbox, but today she saw Jean when she was walking in. Jean has just returned from her trip to the Maldives, and Claire just has to find out all of the details from her trip! She knows that she will never get to the Maldives, so she's prepared to live vicariously through Jean's experiences. She hurriedly leaves little Robbie (as Robert is affectionately called) in the sandbox. It's his first time on his own with the other toddlers.

Robbie looks around at all of the toddlers in the sandbox. He sees the regular gang and a few new faces there. Everyone is doing something with their little portion of the sand. He thinks to himself, "What am I supposed to do? Why am I in this sandbox alone? Should I build something? What if it doesn't look right?" He frantically looks for Mom to come over and help him with his sand, but she is sitting on one of the benches in a very involved conversation with Mrs. Jean. Fearful and nervous, Robbie is unprepared for this situation. He thinks to himself, "Mom can't expect me to build something on my own!" He seems to lack the motivation to build or complete anything until his mom comes back. Feeling indecisive, he notices a stick outside of the sandbox, picks it up and begins to play with it. Then, he notices a leaf in the sand and begins to tear it into little pieces.

Mom's return is taking so long, that Robbie's attention turns once again to the sand. He looks around with curiosity at some of the other children, who are either building castles or making pictures in the sand. Still feeling a bit lost and doubtful of his ability in this situation, Robbie hesitantly squeezes some sand between his fingers. Then he grabs a handful and halfheartedly pushes it around his part of the sandbox. He tries making a few things with it, but then gives up all together. "Maybe I'll wait until Mom comes back," he says again. Meanwhile, the other kids in their areas of the sandbox are still doing something with their sand. He's not sure of what else to do. What a dilemma! Feeling overwhelmed, Robbie takes his handful of sand, slowly raises his hand to his mouth and begins to *eat* the sand! By the time that Robbie's mom returns to check on him there is no sign that he's made any progress in the sandbox.

Robbie's experience in the sandbox reminds me of an [2]anecdote about an entrepreneur who went away on a sabbatical for a year and left his three businesses in the hands of his three most trusted associates. The first associate put together an aggressive marketing plan and increased the profits of that business by 100%. The second associate put together a strategic business development plan that increased the profits of the business by 50%. The third associate shut the business down after the first month. Though he had imagination, he had no drive, he was fearful and consequently did nothing. When the entrepreneur returned home he checked in with the first two associates. As you could guess, he was extremely happy with what they had done. He put them in charge of the new businesses that he had started in the places he travelled to while he was away. He then went to see the last associate, hoping for good news, also. However, in his meeting with the entrepreneur, the associate explained to him how he did not want to lose the business by not having enough clients. So, he shut it down until his boss' return. When the entrepreneur found out what his last associate had (not) done, he was extremely angry and upset with his lack of productivity. This last associate was proof of what fear, lack of focus and drive would cost him. The Entrepreneur then cut off all ties with this associate. The associate who did nothing shows what is at the heart of everyone that eats the sand: Fear, nervousness, neediness and self-destructive/addictive tendencies. When you add these together, creativity and drive are stifled. This associate ate the sand, just as Robert our toddler did.

- **Not sure of the purpose of the sand**

The Eater is not quite sure what to do with the sand so with nervous energy, or out of distraction, he begins to eat the sand. Of course the sand does not taste good, but the feeling of being uncomfortable overrides the logic. So, he eats the sand. The only problem with eating the sand is that it can make you sick.

The things that we fight with internally and lose to, will always show up externally in our behaviors.

The purpose of the sandbox is to explore and show creativity by building things, drawing things and doing something with your sand. The Eater of the sand is not sure what to do. When we do not understand the purpose of something or are afraid of our purpose, then misuse (or abuse) will usually take place. In most cases, the Eater of the sand has not discovered his or her individual purpose or perhaps they are running from their purpose because it scares them. When we run from who we are, we are in essence allowing self-defeating behaviors and habits to form. The behaviors show up as external evidence of the fight that is taking place within us.

- Not prepared

Many failures take place because there was no preparation for success. The Eater does not prepare and do the things necessary to achieve success. They seem to think that things will work out if they are meant to. That may be true sometimes with some things, but very rarely does one arrive at the right destination by chance. To get somewhere specific, it takes discipline, preparation and a plan. Life has opportunities that will come our way but they can and will only be acted upon by those who have taken the time to prepare for those opportunities.

The Eater figuratively "eats up" time and resources until it is too late to respond, and the opportunities have passed their way. Preparing is too much like work and the Eater does not often have the drive to prepare. They feel as if, when the stars are aligned for them, they will all of a sudden just BE! What they fail to realize is, that opportunities are available to everyone. It is only those who are disciplined, and who prepare, that turn opportunities into achievement.

- Needs perfect conditions before stepping out

Some Eaters are waiting for the perfect conditions before they will act or do anything that moves them toward success. They are afraid to act. Eaters tell themselves that once a) the stars are aligned, b) the economy is good, c) there is money in the bank, d) they are married, and e) the dog stops barking, they will then make the move to step out in life and do what is necessary for advancement. The problem with this kind of thinking is that it is excuse - and fear-based and not based on reality. Who knows whether the Eater of the sand would act if situations were perfect?

Situations are rarely perfect, so the Eater of the sand can continue to hide behind the fear of failure, and even fear of success.

The fear of Success for the Eater of the sand is that with success comes change, and with change comes unfamiliarity and discomfort. This can scare an Eater more than the fear of failure. The rut of consistency is a nice, comfortable place where they have been for so long that it is the only place that they feel at home. The longer that they remain complacent with inactivity, the harder it is to move. Movement seems almost impossible, even with the best intentions.

One of the biggest injustices is self-deception! Eaters often deceive themselves about what they will do. However, if you listen closely, you will notice that there is no 'when' or 'how' what they will do will be accomplished? If you ask these kinds of questions the Eater will often become agitated and defensive because they know there is no real strength behind their words. They like to talk a good game without actually stepping onto the field.

- Hides, or wastes talents

Eaters are known for hiding their gifts and talents. Because they are unsure of how to get themselves out of their rut of comfort, they often die and are buried with their gifts and talents. The Eaters will sit on their hands and will not use or develop their innate talents. The interesting things about gifts and talents are that they are like muscles; which grow and become stronger with use. However, when gifts and talents are not used, just like muscles – they get smaller and weaker even though they are still there. When the Eater is not comfortable with their gifts and talents, they are usually under the impression that they don't need to exercise them. In addition, they believe that simply having the gifts and talents means they are prepared when opportunities knock. There is nothing further from the truth. For example, when someone has a very talented voice, when they sing it is a lovely thing to hear. If they go without practice they will find that while they can still sing and it may be enjoyable, it is not at its best. The audience and the singer will both be able to tell. This is what is so valuable about the art of preparation and exercising your gifts and talents. A wise man once said that when he is looking for talent in a person, he looks for the person who is already exercising their talent in some area!

The other aspect of the Eater is the one who has not even discovered their gifts and talents. This personality does not believe that they have what it takes to do anything productive. They dig a rut of complacency to hide themselves in. They are not sure what their purpose in life is and they are afraid and unmotivated to find out. Consequently, they spend the majority of their time on timewasting activity. Eaters will switch their focus from what they know that they should do in life to the distraction of entertainment. *There is nothing wrong with entertainment, but too much entertainment robs a person of their potential for creativity.*

Entertainment could be television shows, movies, social media, binge eating, telephone conversations, external activity, etc. Eaters seek entertainment because it makes them feel good for a while. It helps them to take their mind off of themselves, and the empty hole within, that would be filled if they were living in their purpose. The Eater is looking for something to ease their pain while taking their attention from their responsibility.

[1]Responsibility {response-ability} is to respond with your ability. Eaters either do not know or see their own ability. If they did, they would not make excuses for not getting things done. When we make excuses, we are saying that we were unable to respond with our ability. When Eaters do not know their own ability they shrink under pressure and consequently do nothing. Everyone has been given some type of ability. But not everyone uses what they have been given. Some may have more ability than others but we all have some. One way to know for sure that you have ability is when you are handed responsibility. *Responsibility only presents itself to those who have the ability to handle it.* You will find that those with a lot of responsibility have proven their ability to handle more. More is always given to those who have the ability and use it.

- Unsure of themselves

Eaters are unsure of themselves. At the heart of the matter is their fear of failure. Because they are lacking in self-esteem and self-confidence, they see things as happening for the worst. When someone lacks confidence in themselves they also lack confidence in their actions. Many times, Eaters of the sand refuse to make a decision…so it is hard to achieve significant progress. Eaters doubt themselves. [1]Doubt means to waver, to hesitate to believe and to distrust. *To doubt others is one thing but to doubt oneself is to live in a prison that you have erected yourself.* Eaters constantly second-guess themselves, and even when it is time to make a decision they are not confident that it will be the right one.

Confidence comes from thinking the right thing, and seeing and doing the right things. This gives someone better results and better results lead to greater confidence. This is not to say that when you have confidence you will always make the right decisions, but you tend to make better decisions when you are confident. Your confidence should be based on information that you have obtained and not just your feelings at a particular moment. Good information helps you to make better decisions and better decisions can help build confidence. Many Eaters make decisions based on how they feel. The problem with this kind of rationale is that feelings can change frequently. They are inconsistent. Making decisions based on feelings will also make your life inconsistent. You can go up and down; like a rollercoaster. When you base your decisions on good information rather than feelings' you will live a life that is more consistent and steady. Life is about the decisions you make. The quality of your decisions can create success or reward you with a lot of heartache.

- [1]Sluggard: A person who is habitually inactive or lazy, slow, lacking in energy

Eaters are seen as being inactive, lazy, slow and lacking energy. They lack motivation and drive. Every now and again, they might become slightly active but before long they fizzle out to a place of inactivity. The interesting thing about an Eater is that they will do activities that will require some effort on their part, but when it comes to building something substantial for their lives they become stagnant.

The Sea of Galilee is a freshwater lake located in the Middle East. The water running from this sea goes into the Jordan River, which then flows with fresh running water into another sea. The sea that it runs into has no outlet and therefore it is called the Dead Sea. Even with fresh water flowing into it from the Jordan River, the Dead Sea does not allow movement through it. Without movement things become stale and begin to stink. Because the water does not move and is stagnant, it stinks. The Eater's inactivity and inability to focus on life goals will leave them stagnant with a life of regrets, as well as potential memorable moments when they are older.

Oftentimes, Eaters of the sand are looking for others to do their work and build things for them. They begin to live vicariously through others. When people want to live vicariously through another, it is because they want to associate with victory and success. In the case of the Eater, they either think that they do not have any ability or they just don't use it. So as a way to feel victorious in life, they live through another. They enjoy associating with greatness rather than living out their own greatness.

- **[1]Procrastinator: One who defers action, delays and puts off doing something, especially out of habitual carelessness or laziness**

The Eater is comfortable with procrastination. It is a rut of behavior. There are times when the Eater knows what they are supposed to do and yet they still end up eating the sand. To procrastinate is to defer action, and put things off until the next day or even never. Action is delayed from day to day and then something comes up that causes the action to be put off once again. So, procrastinators do not produce with consistency. When you really want to do something you will make the time to get it done. When you really don't care one way or the other you will allow things to get in the way. *Procrastination is a slow and numbing way to death, while you are still alive.*

Two common traits of Eaters of the sand are: a lack of focus and determination, and being easily distracted (deterred). *If you don't determine how your day will turn out, you will let the day determine it for you.* If an Eater really wants to get over the procrastination habit, they will have to be diligent and unafraid to allow life to determine the way things will be. It will be difficult, but it can be done. It will start with The Eater making better decisions. An Eater has the potential to be a consistent producer. Producers are fruitful and make good things happen.

- **Addictive behaviors**

Addictive behaviors are often a sign of an internal struggle in an individual. The habits that most Eaters of the sand form almost always work against them. These behaviors become addictive because it takes their attention away from the struggle within themselves. Eaters of the sand often put aside big dreams because they don't believe or see how they can be accomplished. So they 'medicate' themselves with habits and behaviors that become addictive and are at an abusive level, e.g., overeating, drinking, drugs, medications, shopping and excessive entertainment. When we hurt in one area and refuse to address the pain or the injury, we often overcompensate in other areas. This is true – both physically and emotionally. When this overcompensation takes place emotionally, it often births an addiction of some sort. So we do something that makes us feel better, but it is only a distraction from the real issue.

- **Having a relationship with an Eater**

The best thing that you can do for an Eater is encourage them and give them some concrete steps to follow. This will help them to have confidence in their ability to move forward and to make some progress. Telling them about their faults will not help the situation at all. Pointing out their behavior will only cause them to be defensive and will only make them reluctant to open up to you anymore. More often than not, doing that will cause them to stay trapped in the behavior rather than helping to free them. The Eater is often very aware of their limiting behavior but they feel stuck in a rut. The complacency of being in a comfortable place makes it hard to decide to move toward getting out.

Most Eaters waste (eat up) their time, or have their priorities mixed up. You can help them by suggesting how to prioritize, (i.e. things that should be done first and perhaps helping them to organize their day). Also, having a goal that you can both work toward together with a timeline and priorities will help as well. You may end up doing most of the work on a joint project, but at least it helps the Eater to see the correct method (of preparing, prioritizing, and action) that should be used when obtaining a goal. Also, do something that is of interest to the Eater, and you will have more of a chance of having their participation. Remember that inwardly, Eaters need to discover something worth living, moving, and changing for…something that gives them meaning. This should encourage and inspire them toward seeing, and achieving a goal, and ultimately their destiny.

Strengths and Challenges of an Eater Personality

Strengths: Articulate, Bright, Talented, Great Meaningful Purpose

Challenges: Procrastination, Laziness, Uncertainty, Fear, Addiction.

Chapter Three

The Crusher-Hater

A soul filled with jealousy, envy and pride cannot see truth.

"Crush what you're Building in the Sand" Personality

Mike is 3 years old, and he is going to the park just up the street from his house. He has been to the park several times, but today will be his first time playing in the sandbox without Mom's or Dad's supervision. Mike doesn't really know how to play with others without there being some kind of adult intervention. Today is the big day. His parents are really looking forward to letting their son play in the Sandbox by himself. Once they put Mike into the sandbox, with the other children, they take a seat on a nearby park bench. At first everything seems fine. However, after just a short period of time, his parents painfully watch from the distance as Mike steps on, kicks, and destroys what the other children have been building with their sand.

Mike's story reminds me of the [2]story of the man who had four wives who bore twelve sons. The sons were very competitive with each other, just as the wives were in competition for their husband's attention (not a formula that I recommend). One of the sons had a dream that he would be a great ruler one day, even over his family. When he awakened and shared the dream with his father and brothers, they were infuriated with him and his dream of success. Their first thoughts were, *you will not be greater than us even if you are dad's favorite*! That dream became a source of contention between the competitive brothers.

One day, while all of the young men were away from home, they plotted to destroy their youngest brother – and ultimately, his dream. So they dropped him into a pit, hoping that he would suffocate. Before they left him for dead, they saw a group of merchants passing by. Instead of leaving their brother in the pit, they decided to - in essence - sell him into slavery as a servant to the merchants. Saying, *"Let's see what becomes of this dreamer and visionary now."* As time progressed, the brother who was now in a foreign land, rose to a position as a powerful government figure. He was in a place of power in a nation that had plenty of substance during a time of famine. Just as he had dreamed, his brothers had to come to this nation for provision and they were bowing before him to get the provisions that they needed.

A Crusher, or Crushers in this case – being visionless or having tiny dreams – become jealous, and begin to exhibit destructive behaviors, when faced with others who have dreams of accomplishing things. Crushers feel that by destroying what others are doing, they can feel better about what they have or have not accomplished. This is what happened in the case of Mike in the sandbox, and the sons who turned on their own brother.

- Jealous

When Mike is put into the box to play with his sand he becomes unhappy and angry after a while, because he allows himself to compare his work to the other kids in the sandbox. Mike is what we call a Crusher/Hater. This is a term that is used to describe someone who is jealous. [1]Jealousy is a feeling of resentment against another because of their perceived success or advantage. Perhaps when Mike played by himself, or in his parents' presence, he didn't need to compare himself to anyone else. However, there are now other kids in the box and he doesn't have any buffers. Jealousy can occur when people compare themselves with others. The comparison is usually about external factors, like how people look, their accomplishments, or accumulations.

If we look at Mike as our example we will see that when he was put into the sandbox, he discovered some things about himself that he did not like. In an effort to feel better about himself he decides to tear down what others were doing. Crushers can't handle being around others that they perceive are just as or more successful than themselves. While in his mind he may think it is leveling the playing field, he is exhibiting destructive behavior and destroying what someone else has created. This is what Crushers do. Because of this, they will often hang around others that will look up to them and where they feel like the big shots. Also, like the brothers in the story, Crushers are not people that you want to share your dreams, visions and goals with, because they are not happy with themselves. *Crushers carry hate because they usually find it hard to love themselves.* Therefore, hate comes naturally. They will try to destroy your dreams and aspirations with their negative words and/or actions. As a great man once said, [3]"there is something not quite right about someone who needs to pull someone else down, in order to feel better about themselves." *Politicians take note.*

- **Fault finders**

Crushers are fault finders. They are not happy with what they have accomplished in life and will discourage others from pursuing their dreams by finding fault with the people, or with their plans. There are times when you need the opinions of others about different endeavors, but make sure you do not only consult with a Crusher. A Crusher will give you more reasons to <u>not</u> following through than reasons to pursue your goals.

I remember being at a Christmas party with my wife a few years ago. When it was time to leave I left with a couple (Mr. and Mrs. X) and a few others while my wife gathered a few of her things. As we went to the elevator and waited for it to arrive, an attractive young lady came out of one of the apartments and waited with us. As soon as Mrs. X saw her she decided quietly to rip her apart with insults. I was embarrassed that she could say things about someone that she did not know. My wife then came and joined us not knowing what was said and began to compliment the woman on her clothing and how nice she looked. As we all exited the elevator, Mrs. X continued finding fault with the young lady and hurling insults. She, unknowingly, disclosed to us her insecurities and that she was a Crusher.

- Super-critical

Crushers are super-critical, judgmental, and can be derogatory. They tend to have a self-righteous attitude and believe that they can do things better than others. Crushers don't like to be outdone; therefore, when confronted with others who have achieved success, they are critical. A Crusher will find something wrong with another to boost their own self-image. The basis for this critical behavior is a really poor self-image. Crushers don't like what they see when they look inwardly, so they look outwardly at others to find real or perceived cracks, flaws, and weaknesses. Targeting the negative things in others helps to justify their own negative actions and mindset of believing that they are better in some way than others. This poor self-image often leads to a very unhealthy, super-critical mindset which creates a negative lifestyle.

- Threatened by your success

Your success has a way of bringing Crushers and haters to the surface. As long as they see themselves on your level and that you are not outdoing them, they are perfectly fine with you. But, just as soon as you become more successful or prosperous than the Crusher/Hater thinks you should be, then they become your hostile judge and jury. Crushers may even seem sympathetic when you are going through a rough period in life. They may even seem understanding, but inwardly they are happy that a perceived failure has taken place in your life. *Your failures make them comfortable but your success threatens them.* Seeing others succeed becomes a constant reminder of their own failure and lack of drive to achieve the very things that they desire themselves.

- Envy: afraid to admit they desire what you have

Crushers are afraid to admit that they really want what you have. They have not taken the time to figure out how to build and have some of the things that you have. Pride which runs hand and hand with fear, keeps them from obtaining success. Pride tells them that they don't need any help, and that they don't have to ask any questions (because they feel like they know it all). Actually, they only know what has led them to the point they are at right now. Asking questions and walking in humility are also perceived as weaknesses. The Crusher will put on a mask to cover up the real person on the inside. With such a poor self-image, they do not want others to see them in the way that they see themselves. The fear of being seen as weak and incomplete causes a puffed up exterior which portrays an image that is not on their internal landscape. Crushers have not figured out that *in order to grow, you have to know.* Acting out in anger and strife, causes them to destroy what they feel most threatened by – your success.

- **Not sure what to do or what to build with their sand**

Crushers in a sandbox are not sure of what to do with their sand. In addition, sometimes when things are built with their sand, it doesn't seem to last. More often than not, they build something but it does not come out the way that they expected. Disappointment leads to bitterness about the situation and also with anyone who is doing better than they are. Crushers are usually trying to tear down what others are building because in their lives disappointment and failure has caused them to give up. They look at what others have done and begin to compare their sand with others. Comparison is like running a race and looking sideways at your opponent. Sooner or later you are going to trip up! A wise man once said that [3]comparison is a fast track to misery. When we understand what our sand is supposed to look like, then we won't get caught up with what others are building because we know that we are doing what we are supposed to do. It is difficult for a Crusher, having a blurred vision of themselves, to clearly see how or what they are supposed to build. If you don't see yourself properly, then it will be difficult to understand the purpose for the sand and what you need to build. The purpose for being in the sand is discovered only when Crushers discover who they really are. Comparison, envy and tiny thinking will not lead to that discovery.

- **Unable to reach their destination**

Imagine that you were invited to a party and you really want to go. So you get in your car and start to drive there but can't find the address to the party. For some reason, your directions are wrong and you spend all of your time trying to get to the party but do not get there. Everyone is at the party having food, drinks, enjoying good music and company but you can't get there because you are lost. You pull over to the side of the road in frustration. Sometime later, you see people who are on their way home from the party and they tell you what a great time they had. Although your directions were wrong, you were too afraid and prideful to ask for the right directions and you missed out on everything.

This is what it is like for a Crusher. They desire to reach success but they are unable to reach the destination. They drive around for hours, days, and even years trying to get to a destination that they are unable to reach. Frustration begins to set in and now they begin to resent and hate the ones who have reached their destination. Simply put, your success reminds them of their failure. Consequently, they end up driving around for hours, days, years and, yes, decades unable to reach their destiny.

- Desire for control

Fear causes Crushers to want to be in control. They feel like they are in control when they are tearing down or destroying something that someone else has or is trying to build. *A desire for control causes more destructive behavior than anything else.* We were not designed to control other people. We were built to have control over ourselves when we meet adverse situations and circumstances. Humans were not created to dominate each other, and trying to dominate another person will only lead to strife. Strife leads to confusion which also causes one's vision to be blurred. ¹Confusion actually means lack of clarity or distinctness.

Crushers – in their desire to be in control and dominate others – cannot see situations as they really are. They spend their time hating, instead of building. Crushers want to control others because they lack self-control. When control is not taken internally first (self-control) the Crusher will try to take control externally; of people and surroundings. Control gives most people a sense of safety. When we don't have control we feel vulnerable. The way that the Crusher approaches the issue of control of people and surroundings, versus an average person, is very different. It is a rather intense experience. What Crushers do not understand is that self-control allows a person to have peace of mind when external circumstances change. The Crusher's purpose and vision for the future will continue to elude them until they begin to show self-control over their thoughts, words and actions. This is how true strength is built, not in the control of others – but of self!

- **Poorly developed awareness of their own talents and gifts**

Because Crushers are self-reliant and don't like to ask for help, they often stop learning. Successful people who are mature realize that the biggest key to their success is learning. Once you stop learning you stop growing. Being self-reliant stops Crushers from developing and growing. Many times they are not even aware of their own talents and gifts that they possess. They are blinded and preoccupied with what others have and what others are doing. They don't spend much time looking within, because introspection is uncomfortable and can cause disappointment. So, their talents and gifts go unnoticed. They also go uncelebrated.

There are times when Crushers are aware of their talents and gifts. However, they allow pride to get in the way, because they become so preoccupied with their gifts, that they have a hard time building anything. Due to the improper use of focus and immaturity, they experience a hard time in focusing on the sand in their hands and what they are required to build. This is the other side of the reason for a lack of progress. In spite of having great potential and being quite capable, they can't seem to make their talents and gifts work for them. Again, the irrational fear that others might be better, more talented and gifted than them accounts for the lack of progress. So when they see others using their talents and gifts they begin to hate and crush what others have built, and are doing.

- Background of Anger

Anger is what lurks in the background of a Crusher. When a Crusher does not do or give their best to attain their best, they get angry at the results that others get – the results they feel like they should be able to attain. The desire to want to hurt or crush someone or something has a dangerous negative element behind it called anger. Anger, when unchecked, can escalate to rage and then to what is called a 'red zoned' case. A red-zone Crusher is toxic in relationships and their behaviors must be avoided. Their anger is like being intoxicated. It causes all rationale to leave and sure destruction will result.

[2]There were two brothers who made gifts for their father. One brother bought him a beautiful gift that the father really enjoyed. The other made him a gift from things that

he had leftover, and it was not really as appealing. The father enjoyed the gift that was beautiful but did not care for the gift made with leftover material. The brother who gave the lesser gift began to look at his brother who gave the better gift as being his problem. He told himself that if his brother were not around then his gift would have been accepted by his father. After days of feeling angry and inadequate, he murdered his brother so that he could wipe away the reminder of his brother's success. That is extreme – by any type of reasoning!

Instead of the brother – the murderer – giving a better gift, he became preoccupied with his brother; thinking that he was the problem. As you can see, his anger escalated to rage and then violence and led him to kill his brother, simply because his own works were disappointing. With Crushers, the mindset is: *I hate you and your works because they remind me that I have not given my best.* This is an extreme case, but hate and anger unchecked will simply grow. Many people are Crushers and don't realize it. They often have problems with other people because of the results that those people have obtained.

- Having a relationship with a Crusher

Having a relationship with a Crusher can be very challenging. If you are perceived as being or becoming more successful than a Crusher, then you will have to put up with jealousy, envy, criticism and destructive behaviors from them. Often, you can be in a relationship with a Crusher and not know it until you begin to show signs of success. Once the signs of success start to show up, then the Crusher begins to show their true colors. The Crusher fears that you might outgrow them if you become more successful than them. The Crusher personality has always been there during your relationship. However, you might have missed the warning signs because the hate was not directed toward you until you became successful or had a dream.

When a Crusher becomes aware, or their own purpose or vision is made known to them, they can begin to live life with meaning. While you cannot discover someone else's purpose for them, you may be able to help by getting them to talk about their own dreams and aspirations. In addition, you can help them find out what their detractors have been. More than likely, you will find out that something happened that stopped them from really pursuing their dream. This process could lead to some positive and painless introspection and cause them to move forward in a more positive way. You can also be positive when the Crusher is being negative. At first, this will feel to them like you are skinning them with an apple peeler. In the relationship, you can be an encourager and celebrate their progress and success. Hang in there and you should see a difference by being a positive influence.

Strengths and Challenges of a Crusher Personality

Strengths: Passionate. Driven. Talented. Gifted.

Challenges: Envious. Critical. Destructive. Angry. Negative thinker. Frustrated.

Chapter Four

The Pooper

Many herds have run off the cliff because of panic within the herd, caused by one.

"Poop in the Sand" Personality

Ben and Jeremy are toddlers playing in the sandbox. They just built a moat around the castle and now they are building a fort together. Along comes little Johnny who is a new toddler to the sandbox. Johnny's mother sets him down in the sandbox, but she stays close by him. She knows enough about Johnny that she cannot, or does not believe that she can move too far away from him. As long as he can remember, Johnny has been overprotected and has felt secure from being close to those that he is familiar with. Mom sees Kathy, her friend from college, as she walks by with her dog, not too far away. She takes a quick jog in her direction, while calling her name. Kathy turns around and then they hug and begin catching up on old times. Mom is close enough to monitor Johnny as she carries on her conversation with Kathy. Johnny looks at his mom then looks for a long time at Ben and Jeremy who are playing happily together. They are unfamiliar to him. That is uncomfortable. He feels the sand in his hands and it does not feel comfortable. After a few minutes of analyzing his situation and exploring the feelings that are uncomfortable, Johnny begins to cry loudly. His crying escalates to panic, when, after such a high level of fear causes him to lose control of his bodily functions. Oops! He poops in the sand!

Johnny's situation reminds me of a [2]story about a young man and his friend who were searching for his father's lost horses. During that time, his fellow countrymen were looking for a new king to lead their nation. The young man and his friend somehow found themselves in front of a Prophet, who told the young man that *he* had been selected to be King! The Prophet instructed him to go back to his father's house and wait for his inauguration as the new king of the nation. However, on the day that the Prophet arrived at the location for the inauguration, the young man could not be found. They finally found him hiding behind the farm equipment and machinery. This was supposed to be a day that he was going to be appointed as king, but instead he was hiding. He found himself in a situation that was meant to be favorable, but it was overwhelming to him, so he panicked and went into hiding.

What a situation! Johnny's behavior is just like that. In a new and overwhelming situation, he hides behind things that are familiar and/or makes a mess. This behavior stems from a poor internal self-image and not adapting to change.

Sometime after the inauguration this young (new) king was preparing the nation for battle against their enemies. He was filled with fear and all those in his army, who followed him, were also fearful. The Prophet therefore instructed the king to meet him in a certain city at a certain time so that he could offer a sacrifice on the king's behalf before the battle began. In those days, the only one who could offer a sacrifice was the Prophet. When the Prophet was not there on time, the king decided to offer a sacrifice anyway. This was strictly prohibited and the king knew it. He chose to operate in fear, impatience and panic, and made a big mess of things. He ultimately lost his position and status as king, because of his hasty and fear-based decisions.

- Making a mess

I think we all know someone who makes a mess out of just about everything that they are involved in, when they are in a crisis. There are some of us who may even walk behind them with a "Pooper-scooper" in hand – cleaning up the messes they make. Some of us may work with, or for a

Pooper. Poopers are not really secure or patient individuals, and because they are insecure they become alarmed when they are unfamiliar with surroundings and/or procedures or are under pressure. Oftentimes, they may make decisions that waste a lot of time and effort. Poopers also tend to primarily look at the negative side of a situation instead of what can be done to positively address the issue at hand. Even though a Pooper may be in a position of authority, he or she will approach situations with the same thought process and methodology.

Poopers tend to escalate situations or issues very quickly. In the Pooper's thinking, they are striving for what seems to be order. But, unfortunately we live in an age when things don't always go according to plan and a world where things are sometime out of order. Every issue cannot be approached with the same methodology. It is the lack of familiarity or perceived order in circumstances that causes a Pooper to become overwhelmed and discombobulated with what seems like disorder.

- •Uncomfortable in new settings

Poopers flourish, or operate at their highest level of efficiency and productivity when they are in an environment that creates security. This would be familiar people, practices or surroundings. They are uncomfortable and find it difficult to function in new environments. Many times this is what causes a Pooper to shine one moment and then have a dim outlook the next. Poopers are loners, for the most part, who feel like they have more control when things stay the same in their environments – including relationships. They actually make a very committed partner. Poopers prefer not to do anything out of the ordinary. They like to play it "safe." They will watch the same shows, eat the same foods at the same restaurants, and drive the same route to work. They become programmed in a routine and will not want to venture out of their comfort zones.

•Being immature in times of pressure

Life is about challenges, trials, tests and pressures. Poopers have a very difficult time with pressure because they have not matured to a level of thriving outside of their comfort zone. They are comfortable when things are "normal." It usually does not take much out of the ordinary to put them in panic mode. When a Pooper is uncomfortable they tend to have a short attention span and do not pay attention to details. It is not uncommon to give the simplest of multiple directions to a Pooper and have them get totally mixed up and become incapable of carrying the directions out. They have not taken the time to develop mentally and socially, to be able to cope with change. If given the chance to embrace change they would rather run, and remain detached, than stretch and gain new methods of coping. Embracing change is a normal part of a maturing person's life, but not for the Pooper. Because of their unwillingness to embrace change, they cannot grow past their 'pooping' behavior. Therefore, pressures and changes keep them trapped in the same behavior.

•Following familiar patterns

If you are in any way associated with a Pooper, then understanding how a Pooper is wired, and how they process things is a must. Poopers tend to follow patterns that have been successful for them in the past. Routines create security. Their reactions are usually very predictable because they are creatures of habit. Habits – good or bad, give them a sense of normalcy, control and security. While we are all creatures of habit, to some degree, the Poopers take habits and routines to a whole new level.

Habits are like a compact disc (CD) that has your favorite song. Whenever you play that CD you will hear your song, the same way every time, unless there is a scratch (new groove) on the CD. When a scratch causes the song not to play correctly, most people will realize that the CD will need to be replaced. However, the Pooper will try to keep playing the same CD; practicing the same habit. So, when what has always been done (a habit) is now producing a different result, instead of realizing that something has changed, a Pooper will keep doing the same thing to create the original result. The lack of order then creates agitation and panic because things are now unfamiliar. It is at this point that things can become a big mess for the Pooper and for all those involved.

Most Poopers are rigid and very stubborn when it comes to having to change. They resist change like it is the plague. Many Poopers like for things in their homes to be arranged the same way. In some severe cases, some Poopers may even have Obsessive Compulsive Disorder (OCD.)

- **Panicking easily; perceived disorder brings panic and insecurity**

Poopers panic easily when things don't go their way. When things are not the way they want them to be they can resort to threats to get what they want. Because Poopers don't pay attention to all of the details, they can quickly go way off the deep end when it is not necessary.

[1]Panic is defined as *a sudden overwhelming fear, with or without cause, that produces hysterical or irrational behavior, and that often spreads quickly through a group of persons or animals.*

This is why it is extremely important to try as best as possible to manage expectations for the Poopers in your circles/relationships. They can quickly take a calm situation and turn everything into turmoil in a matter of minutes. They can create confusion, frustration and anxiety within your relationship or environment very quickly. *Many herds have run off the cliff because of panic within the herd caused by one.*

•Fearful of the unknown and rejection

Poopers have a deep-seated fear of the unknown. Just the thought of doing something without knowing what the end result will be is terrifying to them. A Pooper's behavior is driven from the insecurity of not feeling confident, strong and positive in earlier stages of their lives. They don't have confidence that they can do the right things, so they don't feel strong or empowered which leads to a negative mindset and actions. Feelings of inadequacy and rejection stem from that negative mindset. This is ultimately the driving force of their behavior. *Their main insecurity is rejection.* They just don't seem to fit in anywhere so they tend to stay by themselves and/or mostly interact with others who have the same insecurities/issues that they have.

•Overcoming the fear of change

As discussed, Poopers are afraid of change, but it is change that will get them out of the rut that they often find themselves in. In order for the Pooper to change, they will have to build confidence and realize that it is okay to make a mistake. They will have to understand that mistakes are okay as long as they learn from them instead of running from them. If a Pooper wants to change their behavior, they should take small steps. This way they don't become overwhelmed and flustered and quit. Real change is never easy, but it can be accomplished when a person's will is established not to quit.

Overcoming negative things is something that we are all faced with. It is how we handle an adverse situation that determines our maturity and the level to which we can grow as human beings. Being able to adapt to changes and make changes is what builds confidence and strength.

•Afraid to ask for help

Many Poopers don't know how to ask for help. When they find themselves in the middle of a problem they seem to make real hasty decisions that are not usually well thought out. Rather than reach out for help, Poopers prefer to solve the problem without relying on an outsider. They believe that asking others for help would make them feel even more insecure. They fail to realize that, having the right minds around an issue or problem will provide a better chance of finding the right solution. Many times the solo mentality of – *I will take care of it on my own* – gets in their way and often makes things worse. Everyone needs help at some point, and if we are afraid to ask for it we cannot grow. There are obstacles that we will face in life that others have overcome. *It is wisdom to get wisdom.* It would be terrible to want to get to the other side of the river and not ask the gentleman who just built his boat how to do it, or for a ride. Wisdom says, "Get wisdom."

- Poopers in the marketplace

Many might ask, "Why would I want to have a Pooper in my group or business?" Simply put, despite the seemingly negative things that we have highlighted, a Pooper can be a valuable asset to you and/or your organization. You don't need to throw away the baby with the soiled diaper.

Some Poopers manage teams and have extremely high-level positions in the marketplace. You may not even know that you are working with a Pooper until something does not happen according to plan or they are put into a new environment. The new environment can be new procedures, new team members, a change in leadership, and social gatherings. One way to tell for sure that you are around a Pooper is that when there is a major change in process, or something new is introduced to them, then there is usually a big mess to clean up. This is often because someone panicked and made things worse.

Poopers are quite smart and valuable in organizations. When you need to have procedures followed to the "T" and when you need to have directions followed without question, a Pooper may just be the person you need. To get the best out of a Pooper, assign them positions in environments where things don't change that often. They will thrive in this type of environment and can be a huge asset to the team. Truly, everyone has a part to play. If we decide to only work with one group of people we limit our accomplishments and ourselves. If everyone thinks the same way in your group you will lack creativity and stunt the growth of the group and/or organization.

Many times Poopers need extra coaching to positively address their challenges. Coaching should be done before, through and after the change. When coaching a Pooper it is best to introduce changes a little at a time so as not to overwhelm them. If you are a Director or Manager and you have a Pooper as a direct report, try your best not to put them in situations that are fast-paced and where change occurs frequently. If you do, you will spend a great deal of your time doing clean up. Instead, put Poopers where they tend to thrive; in situations where strict procedures are followed. Remember that reassuring the Pooper does not always work the first time, especially in the midst of what seems like a crisis to them. This is because at that particular time they tend not to listen well.

In an alternate scenario, when you work for a Pooper, then you may have to "manage up." This means that there may be times when you will have the remedy that prevents your VP, Director or Manager from making a mess as they deal with a change in policy, routine, or process. This will be so much better than allowing them to try to solve it themselves. In addition to increasing your value to your boss, you will help maintain the organization's equilibrium.

This was true in my situation. I used to work for a Fortune 500 company, and there was a Pooper that was indirectly over me in the corporate structure. Any time there was an operations issue with a client, all of his direct reports sheltered him from the news for as long as possible. Most of the time, they would remedy the situation and share with him the progress. This made him feel like he was in the loop without having to solve the problem. This is managing up.

•Having a relationship with a Pooper

Having a relationship with a Pooper can be a very challenging thing if you are fast-paced or spontaneous.

Poopers may seem to lack drive and the motivation to do – and be – more, because they are limited in their minds by fear of change. They definitely cannot handle criticism well and this makes having to correct them quite challenging. Poopers are happy with things being consistent. You may look for new and exciting things to do, but they look at those things as not being necessary. Often, they feel this way because your suggestions take them out of their comfort zone.

While having a relationship with a Pooper can be challenging, it can have rewards such as devotion, loyalty, and trust. Poopers are not necessarily bad company. However, beware of making changes too quickly in the relationship, or you will definitely face some obstacles. Since relationships constantly change to meet the needs of those involved, the Pooper may display some discomfort. But it does not have to be a problem. When relationships change for the long term, Poopers will complain. Be prepared to deal with complaining after the change.

Strengths and Challenges of a Pooper Personality

Strengths: Loyal. Devoted. Follows processes and routines to the "T".

Challenges: Needs routine. Panics easily. Makes a mess. Resists change.

Chapter Five

The Thrower

A soul without belief in itself is a soul that will not be able to live above mediocrity.

"Throw the Sand" Personality

Laura and Jimmy are two toddlers in a sandbox in the park. Jimmy was there first, and he is happily making a sand castle on his side of the sandbox. He is so involved with his work he does not even notice that he has a new playmate; so when Laura joins him, he continues making his sandcastle. Laura is not really comfortable with the surroundings and does not know what to do. She can see that Jimmy is working on a castle so she decides to do that as well, and build her own. It's not something that she's very familiar with doing. However, what she builds doesn't look as good as Jimmy's masterpiece, and it's taking a long time. After a few tries, and after things keep falling apart, Laura is now frustrated and irritated. The thing that she builds does not come out the way she would like, and she is NOT happy. She feels out of place in this environment. Sandboxes are a lot different than playing with toys on the floor of her nursery at home.

Laura knows that something is expected of her, but she just doesn't want to put in the work that is required because she's not sure if building something in the sand is what she is good at. She is not sure if she will be able to build anything at all, so she decides to refuse to participate. As a result, Laura takes the sand and does something with it for which it is not intended: She begins to throw the sand! She throws it up in the air. As she pulls the parts of the unfinished castle by the handfuls, she throws them around the sandbox. Laura eventually throws sand in the direction of Jimmy and his castle. Jimmy finally notices this new playmate. Not only was she making distracting noises before, but now she is trying to mess up the really nice castle that he has made so much progress with. As he looks in her direction, he thinks to himself, "What she was working on does not even look like a castle!" "What is she doing?" "What is going on?" Jimmy is thinking what many of us have thought about the "Throwers" we have come in contact with.

As Jimmy turns around to give his full attention to Laura, he gets a handful of sand thrown right in the front of his shirt. He has to try to defend his castle against this new kid who is having a fit in the sandbox. Laura is happy that Jimmy is paying attention to her, even though he looks really upset about having sand on his shirt! Maybe he will pay attention to her now, she thinks…and she won't have to worry about building anything else in the sandbox.

- What do I do with the sand?

Laura started out trying to build in the sandbox and then became disinterested because she did not see what she wanted to see. A lack of focus or satisfaction with progress caused Laura to stop building altogether. She may have even looked around to see what others were building and compared it to what she had or had not accomplished and quickly became discouraged.

The comparison begins to feed a sense of insecurity and displeasure. Throwers of sand don't believe that they are capable enough. When that mindset is fed, it leads to distracting and potentially destructive behavior. Throwers begin to do things with the sand that was not the original intent -- such as throwing the sand. The problem with this is that there are others in the sandbox and they can potentially get hurt by the sand that is being hurled in their direction.

- Why should I take things seriously?

The perspective of "I am inadequate," (insecurity) coupled with not having things their way, fuels the Thrower's penchant for not taking things seriously. It may be easier to hide behind a joking, let's have fun, why be serious façade, than to really deal with the issues. Of course, while there is nothing wrong with having fun and enjoying life, the Thrower takes this way of approaching life to an often dangerous level, because this lifestyle is often a mask that is hiding unmet needs and deep seated insecurities. It is evidence of an imbalance.

It is often hard to have a Thrower take on additional responsibility. Throwers don't particularly want to be accountable to others. Accountability reminds them that life is serious, and commitment is not comfortable. Throwers are about entertaining and being entertained. Much of their lives are spent chasing playfulness and amusement. These things fill the spaces that are left by unmet needs. So, distractions which may seem like fun and entertainment are often used to fill up the lifestyle of a Thrower. As I indicated earlier, there is nothing wrong with having fun in life but everything should have a balance. Throwers are big time wasters without even realizing it. The distractions of life take the place of real accomplishment and focused achievement. However, because it looks like they are doing something, a Thrower is not even aware of time, or life passing them by. Another factor in the Thrower's lifestyle of distractions is seeking a state of euphoria to numb the hurt and insecurities related to their past. Throwers don't want to be reminded of the past hurts. The past represents a place of pain.

Sometimes emotional scars and hurts are worse than physical scars and hurts. While the human body has an automatic built-in healing process, this is not necessarily so with emotional scars and wounds. Carrying around these untreated wounds and scars, leads to imbalance in the psyche <u>and</u> the body. When emotional healing is not allowed to take place or emotional wounds are hidden, we begin to overcompensate in other areas.

For instance, if I had a bad wound on my arm and did not allow it to heal properly, I would use my other arm more to compensate for things that my wounded arm could not do. The same thing happens emotionally, except that we don't see the wound physically. So we cover it up, we tell ourselves that everything is okay, but then lean heavily in other areas to compensate for what is not healed. In compensating, we pick up behaviors and habits that are not always beneficial. In the case of the Thrower, life becomes filled with distractions, lack of commitment and very few things are taken seriously.

- I am immature

Throwing the sand is also an outward indication of immaturity that results in thought and action. [1]Immature means *not mature, not ripe, not developed, not perfected,* etc. It also means *emotionally undeveloped; juvenile; childish.* Immaturity in adults is typically a sign of mental and emotional hurts that never healed and result in childlike behavior. When a Thrower is put into a serious situation, they often resort to playfulness and jesting. This type of behavior brings them comfort… at least for the moment. While this behavior seems inappropriate to those who are more mature, to the Thrower these actions seem like the appropriate and comfortable thing for them to do. They will be incapable of understanding the mature person's point of view, and will often say that the mature person is way too serious. *A person who is emotionally underdeveloped will not understand a mature person's perspective.*

Because a Thrower's lifestyle is comprised of juvenile thought and behavior, they will tend to attract emotionally volatile and dramatic situations (drama). As a matter-of-fact, the Thrower's life usually has at least one situation going on with drama almost constantly. It is the drama that acts as the catalyst for them to live up to their names as a Thrower. They will often find themselves in situations that expose who they are.

Throwers tend to function comfortably in situations of confrontation and drama, and are willing to accept their role as "the Thrower," engaging in actions where they feel comfortable *literally* throwing! For example, a Thrower can throw physical objects, slash someone's tires, break things, throw punches, have tantrums, throw the blame, and throw accusations. They don't tend to reason and discuss things in a rational way. They prefer not to handle things in an adult manner. Immaturity is their master.

- I want things my way

Throwers always have a justification for their behavior. They have not figured out how to deal with unmet expectations, confrontation, and not having their way. In the marketplace and in relationships, when Throwers don't feel like things are going their way, they will also sabotage the environment.

Many of us have heard of employees leaving or being asked to leave and while they are still there they destroy, damage or disrupt the workplace or co-workers. This is not just limited to physical damage. This is the Thrower's mentality. When things do not go their way they feel a need to retaliate, and get even. Also, if things are not working for them, then they begin to disrupt everyone else's lives. Remember when Laura is in the sandbox and starts to throw the sand? Just as it affected Jimmy, throwing the sand will affect the lives of everyone else who is working/building in the sandbox as well.

- I am throwing a temper tantrum

Throwing the sand is the way that the Thrower chooses to express unhappiness with situations and people. This is their version of a temper tantrum; to let everyone know that they are unhappy. When the Thrower is unhappy the world needs to know about it, and definitely those who are in the immediate area will know it. Throwing things causes damage, and a Thrower gets a thrill from that activity. Throwing seems to release the anger and pent-up feelings of hurt and it makes them feel good to release these things. This behavior becomes a type of trap; nothing has been resolved and unresolved issues will continue to circulate in the Thrower's life indefinitely. So, as long as the issues continue unresolved, the Thrower remains trapped in their behavior. They continue to feel the need to release emotional things through physically and emotionally destructive action. Until another more productive and mature way of dealing with unresolved issues is established, throwing to release anger and pent-up feelings will continue as a behavior.

- I am easily frustrated

Throwers can be emotionally unstable and are often easily frustrated. They may be given to emotional outbursts and may also become loud or threatening. Throwers throw the sand because they feel the need to get the pressure off of them. As a result of being easily frustrated, they quickly blame others for things not working as they expected. Throwing is their way of casting the blame. The damage caused to others by this behavior of throwing sand does not seem to faze them, because relieving themselves of the pressure of being responsible is worth the damage that the other person receives, or is left with.

This reminds me of the [2]story of an ancient king who had many war victories to his credit, until a young warrior joined his army and allowed the king to have ten times the victories over his enemies. This king was grateful for this young warrior's victories because his kingdom and influence increased. Things were going well. However, one day the king returned from a battle and heard the women singing songs within his palace gates to celebrate how the new young warrior had killed tens of thousands compared to the king's thousands. The king, in a fit of jealousy, took a spear and threw it at the young warrior. Thankfully, the young warrior was skilled enough to dodge the weapon. Then, out of respect and fear for the king, he left the kingdom. The king was still so upset about the public acknowledgment of the young warrior that he threw a javelin at his own son, who questioned his behavior.

Laura may not have been trying to kill Jimmy in the sandbox but she was harboring the same mindset as this envious and misguided king. Laura allowed anger, rage and feelings of inadequacy, to fuel her bad behavior of literally throwing things. She was insecure in who she was and does not understand her purpose, or the purpose of the sand.

- I am seeking attention

Throwers are attention seekers. Throwing fits and loud outbursts often get them the attention that they need. As mentioned before, volatile and emotionally charged situations, i.e., drama – is the atmosphere in which the Thrower feels comfortable. This feeds their immaturity and their insecurities. To them, drama is supposed to be a part of the relationship even though it makes others uncomfortable. They tend to attract drama partially because they feel like they have a right to express their displeasure, and throw, if things don't go their way. They know that when they decide to throw something, it will result in people paying attention to them. Even though this is negative attention, it is still attention. Throwers are often jealous of others who are getting attention and will attempt to take the attention from them, even if it means behaving badly.

- I don't believe in myself

A result of the insecurities in the Thrower's mind is the lack of purpose. The insecurities come from not knowing what they are supposed to do in life and the resulting envy of others who do. These insecurities result in the fear of the unknown (having no control) and feeling like a failure. In a dreadful cycle, the Thrower continues throwing in an attempt to satisfy their insecurities. So, insecurity becomes their teacher and fear-based actions continue. Because they have lived with these insecurities for so long, when an idea or opportunity comes to them to move toward a positive way of life, they quickly dismiss the idea because they don't believe that they can achieve it. They often live a life that is far below their real potential, even to the point of ignoring their natural given gifts and talents. They have allowed insecurities and fear to rule them for so long that they have often given up hope of ever truly believing in themselves. *A soul without belief in itself is a soul that will not be able to live above mediocrity.*

Throwers, like Takers also have a deep desire for control. As discussed earlier someone who is truly in control can control his or her own actions, yet this is not the case with the Thrower. A Thrower feels a sense of control, and very powerful when they are throwing, yet it is actually because they are out of control that they are exhibiting the throwing behavior. The behavior gives them a feeling of power even though it is negative and fed by insecurities. Throwing is what they know how to do. They feel like they are in control but it is far from true.

- Having a relationship with a Thrower

A Thrower does not like to be outshined. Throwers often exhibit possessive and jealous behaviors and want to be known as the best. The success of others is often threatening and brings feelings of envy, because they have not discovered their own purpose.

Although you might have what seems like a good relationship with a Thrower, it may not have the depth that you expect. If you try to add trust and responsibility to the relationship you will most likely be disappointed. While you can spend time with them and feel like you enjoy the time that you share with them, you may be surprised to find that you merely have a surface relationship. You may laugh, have great fun with them and have the time of your life but your relationship just can't seem to grow because they lack accountability and trustworthiness. They can intentionally and subconsciously sabotage their relationships that require too much of them.

At the same time, Throwers tend to be highly emotional and they are very loyal to the ones that they love. Yet, if for some reason they do not feel that the same loyalty has been shown to them, they can hurt those they love, by throwing blame, excuses, accusations, punches, and even objects. They feel the need to get back at others and to express their anger in a way that will punish others for what they perceive as being mistreated. Throwers will often give to others but expect to be given back on the same level or more. They keep a running 'tab' of things that they have done for others.

When it is their time to collect on the favors and various things they have bestowed, Throwers expect repayment without any excuses -- they are not usually responsible, and do not take the things that are important to you seriously. When their expectations are not met they become easily agitated and angry and want to throw. They will throw tantrums, become distrustful, throw dishes, etc. A Thrower even reserves the right to throw in the towel on the relationship. A Thrower wants revenge when things don't go their way and will express this through bad behavior. Bad behavior never resolves issues and cannot resolve any issues that a Thrower may have.

* I would like to add that if you are in a relationship where there is physical abuse, that you seek to get out of that relationship as quickly and safely as possible.

Strengths and Challenges of a Thrower Personality

Strengths: Fighter, Strong willed, Courageous, Passionate (feel very strongly about their beliefs)

Challenges: Poor Communicators, Emotionally unstable, Insecure, Jealous, Easily frustrated, Immature, Selfish.

Chapter Six

The Complainer

When someone chooses to feed on negativity, their natural succession is to become bitter.

"Complain about the Sand" Personality

Sarah, the Nanny, brings Jacob to the park on Tuesday to play in the sandbox. She puts Jacob in the sandbox next to the other children and gives him a plastic shovel and a small plastic bucket so that he can play. Once Sarah sees that he is comfortable, she goes off to sit with the other nannies and watches him from a distance. Jacob begins to play in the sand with his shovel and bucket, mimicking what he sees the others doing with their shovels and buckets. As Jacob builds his sandcastle, he notices that his shovel and plastic bucket look like they have been chewed on by Barney – his six-month old golden retriever! Also, his castle does not look like some of the ones being built by the other children. His castle does not have the form and stability of the other sandcastles! An agitated Jacob begins to cry, whine and then wail loudly, because he is really upset about his circumstances. Sarah, and everyone that she's chatting with, can hear his distress. Sarah tries to console Jacob, but to no avail.

They return the next day, and Sarah puts Jacob in the sandbox with a shiny new red shovel and a new red plastic bucket. Jacob begins to build another castle like the day before, but this time he is well prepared with his new tools. Excitedly, he begins to pack the sand into his bucket, but when he turns the bucket over his sand structure does not stay together. It is still lopsided. After a few tries, it is still difficult for Jacob to build a structure like the other children. He changed his shovel and bucket, so why isn't his structure working? He realizes that the sand did not stay together because it was not wet. Jacob overhears Sarah talking with the other grown-ups about how the children who were there earlier in the day had water and they were able to wet their sand so that the sand would stay together.

Now he begins to complain to the other kids, saying if only Sarah had not bought him to the park later in the day so that he could have used some of the water too! It's all her fault! So, it's not too long before there is a complete repeat of the day before. Jacob begins to cry, and whine, and wail! *Poor thing…in his mind, he can't seem to catch a break…*

While many of us may complain from time to time, Jacob (the Complainer) complains almost constantly. This is a habit, not "just an every now and then" thing.

- Murmur -- a condition and sound of the heart

The Complainer can let out a sound that can quickly become unbearable. When you are in the company of a Complainer, they do not usually see the good, only the negative. [1]A heart murmur is an abnormal sound that the heart makes. When a person murmurs, they are complaining and they expose that something is wrong at the heart of the matter (with them.) Complainers are people who have a heart (spiritual heart/soul) matter. Their perspective is off, so they see things wrong which causes them to voice what they see in a way that is negative. When you are around people who always complain it can almost make you feel like you are sick. The constant murmuring makes you not want to be around them. Complainers see so much of what is not perfect or ideal, that they cannot see what is right and good. *When anyone fills up on one thing more than another, they see the thing that is in greater quantity.* Because Complainers have filled up on negativity, they will only be able to see and say the negative. This negativity eats at the soul and often causes other dysfunctions to occur in their lives. Being negative will cause us to have negative expectations and thereby create a negative pattern of events in our lives.

We were not created to carry negativity within us. This is a burden that will only bring about the worst.

- Negative thinking leads to bitterness

Very seldom do Complainers think about others in the sense of helping them. They are usually bitter and not willing to help others. The bitterness comes from always meditating on the negative rather than the positive. *When someone chooses to feed on negativity their natural succession is to become bitter.* "Complainers become bitter about their circumstances, leaving them to think only of themselves and their own needs."

When the Complainer sees others building things and doing things that they were not able to accomplish, they begin to complain and find fault. When they are unable to accomplish a goal, they use complaining about their situations and showing anyone who will listen the reasons why they were not able to obtain the same results.

Their lack of resources, timing, or a person, becomes their scapegoat. In the sandbox, Jacob became upset, the most, when he could see the things that others had built in the sandbox and his building was a disaster. When Jacob allowed envy and jealousy to enter into his heart/mind he opened himself up to the other negative emotions that follow. The same way he opened himself up to envy/jealousy, is the same way that he will have to remedy himself. To close the door to the other negative emotions, he will have to give up envy and jealousy of others. As long as he continues to hold on to these negative emotions, he will be negative and see things from a negative standpoint and therefore he will complain.

- Please be easy

The Complainer would like everything to be easy, or require little effort. The Complainer does not realize that it is perseverance and resistance that builds strength. Things that take little or no effort can be done by anyone. That type of attitude will only allow someone to be average. To have anything that is worthwhile in life, requires much effort on your part. If you do the bare minimum, while hoping for a spectacular result, you are just wasting your time.

- Please work according to my plans

Complainers need everything to work out according to their plan or they will start to give up. Although very few things in life work out perfectly, Complainers are not good with adapting to change or deviation in plan. They do not take into consideration that things may not go as planned. So, when one thing does not go as planned they allow it to mess up the entire day, project, or sometimes their entire life! The attitude of giving up easily and not adapting well to change, makes it easy for Complainers to rehearse – over and over – just how things did *not* go right. This is an excuse and fear – driven approach to life. As a consequence, Complainers begin to caution everyone else not to try things because of all of the wrong things that *could* happen. Though the potential exists for a Complainer personality to shine because of attention to detail and the need for perfection, that same trait can cause Complainers to not get past themselves and the roadblocks that they have allowed to develop in their heart and mind.

- Meet my expectations

When a Complainer's expectations are not met, they quickly proceed with complaining and even look for something else to do. Many Complainers are hurt because they planned for some major things to take place in their lives and they were met with disappointments – sometimes over and over. This has led them to a place of no hope and despair. They have allowed the circumstances to get the best of them and leave them with no spirit to go on. So, many Complainers have quit and have decided not to try anymore and to just accept what life has taught them, "to complain". Complainers see life as having taught them to be safe, don't try, don't get your hopes up because they will only be crushed (by someone or fate). This gives them hope for unmet expectations.

- Excuse-makers for not completing projects

The Complainers in the Sandbox will have 1,001 excuses and reasons why they were not able to complete projects and timelines. Excuses become the Complainer's crutch, so they will take lots of time and go into great detail to explain what went wrong and the reasons why things ended up the way that they did. If a Complainer is really honest with themselves, they would realize that the effort failed in their mind long before they attempted to accomplish the actual goal or project. They were destined to fail because they were only able to see what was wrong and not what was right. Their perspective is obscured by a cloud of negativity.

- Casting the blame and Finger pointing

Complainers are more comfortable with excuses than accountability. They are not willing to take on the responsibility of having failed, so they make excuses and even blame others. When someone is reliable, that person will make sure that things work out one way or another and they can accept blame. While the Complainer is dwelling on what went wrong, a dependable person is using their energy and resources to try to remedy the situation and to make the best of it. I have heard it said that if you aim for the moon and miss, at least you will be out among the stars. The Complainer does not see things this way. They only see the fact that they tried for the moon and did not land there. But when someone positive is in the same situation, they will see the stars and know that they are now *closer* to the moon. Therefore, the next time they launch out, it should land them or bring them closer to the target. Even if they continue to miss they will at least have learned something from their endeavors, which will help with the next launch. The key is that they do not stop trying.

When Complainers don't take responsibility for their effort or lack thereof, they look to shift the blame onto others. Very seldom does the Complainer say that something was their fault. They are usually planning their favorite line, "I told you this was going to happen." Their cautiousness is nothing more than negativity, and a cover-up for not taking responsibility, and passing the blame.

[2]Long ago, there was a tribe of people that dwelt in an uncultured region [in the woods]. The Chief sent a group of the tribe's leaders to go to the plain on the other side of the mountain to see what the land looked like, and to see if it was a place where the tribe could make a new home. The leaders went out into the land and saw the beauty of the

land, the houses, the crops and the opportunity. When they returned, their report to the Chief and the tribe was that the land was beautiful and seemed like a great place to live. They all agreed on this fact, however, ten of the leaders said that there was no way that they could live in such a place. They began to talk about the inhabitants of the land, how strong they were and how big they were. The other two leaders told the tribe that the inhabitants were strong, but valiantly said, "we are stronger than them." However, the two were quickly silenced by the negative report of the ten. The ten saw everything that was wrong with trying to move into a new territory and caused the entire tribe to refuse to move. The tribe was unable to move into the new land while the ten with the negative report were still alive. But, as soon as the ten leaders who saw things negatively died, the tribe was able to possess their new territory and lived well there.

The ten were able to see the good of the new land but their focus quickly shifted to the negative aspects of living there. The negative outlook caused them to see themselves as small and not able to do anything to change their current living situation. Negativity causes you to complain, blame and to shrink back. Negative thinking makes you see impossibilities in your future and therefore cause you to move backward, instead of forward. A person never really stays in the same place for long. Either they move forward or they move backwards.

The two leaders who were able to see the good of the land and to see themselves in a positive way were able to move forward. However, no movement happened until the other ten died in the wilderness. In other words, the negativity in the camp had to die before progress could be made.

- The power of rotating thought patterns, and their results

Complainers rehearse negative thought patterns over and over in their minds. This creates the opportunity for insecurities and negative situations to reproduce quickly. Negative emotions attract negative thoughts just like positive emotions attract positive thoughts. As we experience different situations in our lives, it is easier for us to remember how we <u>felt</u> rather than what we thought. We know that when we are in certain environments we <u>feel</u> a certain way while we may not always remember what we were thinking. *However, it is important to note that just because we do not always remember what we were thinking does not mean that our thoughts carry any less weight.*

Thought patterns that are rehearsed over and over begin to attract like-thoughts. While what we feel seems to come and go, our dominant thoughts remain in the background. *It is what is played in the background of our minds that brings us to the results that we achieve.* The Complainer is filled with negative thought patterns while feeling insecure and begins to speak based on the well-rehearsed thoughts that have been ruminating within them. These rotating thoughts and speech (complaining) begin to produce what has been rehearsed and spoken to the Complainer. So much so, that they must utter their favorite words, "I told you so." They have simply seen the end from the beginning.

This is such a powerful concept that it works the same exact way when the Complainer decides to trade their negative thoughts in for positive thoughts. When the positive thoughts are rehearsed over and over and they have ejected all traces of negative thoughts from the heart/mind, the same process will take place for the ex-Complainer to become positive and see positive results. The positive thoughts replaced, will now begin to have an offspring of more positive thoughts and create positive feelings (security) and positive outcomes.

- Having a relationship with a Complainer

Being in a relationship with a Complainer can just be annoying (LOL!) A Complainer can find something wrong with a beautiful spring day! Your challenge in having a relationship with a Complainer is going to be just that…a challenge. To endure a relationship with this personality, you will need to block your ears from the negativity that is flowing from them. You will have to be the one who sees the silver lining in the otherwise terribly painted, cloudy picture of the Complainer. Complainers tend to be perfectionists, so working on a project with them as the lead can be both challenging and comforting because of their desire for perfection. Being positive and sometimes being silent are two of the best ways to block the negative energy and complaining spirit of these individuals. When Complainers grumble or fuss unnecessarily about a person or situation, you should become accepting and applauding of the good that you see in the person or situation. Show them the other side of their perspective. Stay consistent with doing this, and you will see that their behavior will eventually change or at least change around you.

Complainers look for others to agree with them. So, when you choose to see the other side of things, this will cause them to have to see it as well – or to at least stop complaining in your presence! If they seem to be stuck in a negative frame of mind your optimism may seem irritating… just as you see their complaining ways. Remember you cannot change someone. They must desire to change. You can only show them a better way, not by complaining about them but by being someone who is positive in their presence.

Strengths and Challenges of a Complainer Personality

Strengths: Innate ability to do things in excellence, Organized, Seeks perfection

Challenges: Overly Analytical, Not easily satisfied, Blames others, Blames circumstances, Negative thinker, Noisy, Overly cautious.

Chapter Seven

The My-Sander

It's my way or the Highway.

"My-Sander" Personality

Janice is a pretty and seemingly sweet-natured little girl, until she makes it down to the sandbox and begins to play in the sand. Once in the sand, her outward beauty immediately goes unnoticed as her "My-sand" personality shows her dark and selfish side. It is the "My-sander" personality that is her biggest challenge when Janice is around others. When Janice's mom (Mary) takes a first glance at the sandbox, everything seems to be okay. She sees Janice making a beautiful sand castle. However Mary does not realize, when she placed Janice in the sandbox with the other children, she *immediately* divided the sandbox and its sand into sections. Janice has staked her claim for her share of the sand – declaring that no one else can touch it without there being a problem! The concept of sharing does not enter her mind unless there is something that she can get out of the deal. Janice is an opportunist.

- Silo mentality - don't need "nobody" else

My-sanders can also possess an island, or silo mentality that says that they don't need anybody else. When Janice (the toddler) was playing in the sand, she immediately separated the box into sections and claimed her silo (island). No one could touch her sand or play with it. Other children could give her their sand but once they did, they would need **her** permission to play with it because it is now **hers**! Janice is happy to play by herself or to have others follow along with what she wants to do. If others don't want to play her game, then they can just leave her alone. She is fine with this because at least she gets a chance to do what she wants and that is what makes her happy. It's all about her and her way.

Now as Janice gets older, and she has not matured in this area, she will carry the same mentality into her relationships, i.e., *this is her world and everyone needs to fall in line or fall off.* She finds no real value in others unless they can give her what she wants. The reason she sees no value in others is because she has an unbalanced view of her own value (spiritual net worth). She only sees value in what she possesses because this is what she values. Where her treasures (valuables) are, there will be her heart also.

Janice will become a master manipulator. She will look at different opportunities that others are in (good or bad) for ways to personally benefit. She will display compassion, kindness, and love to get what she wants. <u>My-sanders are calculating opportunists</u>.

- Not Sharing

I would like to clear up the difference between a Taker and a My-sander. A Taker <u>takes,</u> and a My-sander <u>keeps</u> what is theirs and manipulates to get their way. My-sanders are notorious for not sharing. They hold on to stuff; whether it is information, assistance, resources, time, material goods, etc., and even emotions. Selfishness is at the root of this personality. Their motto is, "It is my way or the highway." Sharing is not viewed as a weakness to this personality, it is perceived as a loss. They view sharing like a King would view losing territory or a domain. A My-sander's perspective is that sharing is a loss of goods/ground and or control. So, when My-sanders find themselves in a position of lack, they will often covet *and then manipulate to get* what others have! They usually don't just want a little bit, they like to have it all, because **all** represents full control.

Having full control means that they can call all of the shots and you can live in their world.

- Control issues. Must be in control

People who have to be in control are actually being controlled by *their* desire to be in control. It is a double whammy! It starts with them creating walls and barriers in their lives that they will not allow others to enter. These walls make them defensive and are control mechanisms. An extreme My-sander personality will simply refuse to cooperate and work on projects with others, if it cannot have control. Their effort and participation will be half-hearted, if forced to work with others in the marketplace without having some form of control. What My-sanders don't realize is that *to build anything of significance they will need the contribution of others* which is accomplished by working well with others, sharing, and loosening control.

- Boundaries and barriers – [mental, emotional and physical]

My-sanders have set mental, emotional, and physical 'walls' as a means of defense. In relationships this building up 'walls,' around themselves, will keep others out. They are always in protective or defensive mode. Their attitude is, "It's all about me. I have to protect myself, my needs, etc." Defensive measures are usually necessary when there is a need for security. These unhealthy and unbalanced barriers in their relationships provide a sense of protection and security that protect them from getting hurt. These barriers are also put in place to keep others from getting too close and seeing their vulnerabilities. This gives the My-sander's personality a sense of security; they hold their own fate and will not have to rely on others. It is a fear response. For a My-sander, the fear is of being exposed with low self-image and esteem. Their lives are a façade put together, that keeps outsiders from looking in or getting too close. What the My-sanders fail to realize is, the same walls that keep others out keep them locked in. They stay locked into the same behavior, attitudes and results.

- **Not playing well with others**

My-sanders typically do not play well with others. They want everything their way, and that leaves little room for compromise. In the world of a My-sander, everything is supposed to work for their benefit. This selfish attitude makes it hard for My-sanders to make friends. There are times when they will meet other like-minded people and often experience conflict because other selfish people will have their own needs on their minds. In some cases, there are exceptions -- when other selfish people will understand exactly where the My-sanders mindset is coming from and will form a bond. As you may imagine, this is not a bond that will be deep or built on much loyalty because My-sanders are only loyal to themselves. Usually My-sanders only keep people who are easy to control and/or there to help further their cause, around them. They usually look to allies who can help them accomplish their goals and who are easily discarded after those goals are met. In some cases My-sanders will keep those who are loyal to them around; as long as it is understood that things must work out their way. While My-sanders do not typically get along with everyone, they have a wonderful ability to focus and meet goals. These two traits make them very powerful leaders in one regard, but they are often lacking in other great leader traits, like serving others.

- Possessiveness: "my friends…my time!"

My-sander personalities are possessive about everything! They definitely do not believe in sharing friends. Their friends make them feel comfortable because their roles have been defined and they know what to expect from them. Therefore, My-sanders can feel safe in interacting with their friends. When a new person is introduced into the mix, they feel uncomfortable because this throws the friendship dynamic off – at least in their minds.

This tendency toward possessiveness can often lead to domination of relationships and things. For example, some My-sanders will feel like they have the right to tell their friends who they can be friends with. This type of possessiveness – left unchecked – will lead them to try to dominate their friends in other areas as well. Soon, they will be setting up their schedules, coordinating where they go and with whom, and so on. This possessiveness and need to control through ownership is caused by an emotional imbalance. A My-sander will overcompensate in one area to balance a sense of loss of control in another area. It could be from the loss of something or someone that they held dear. Rather than deal with that pain again, they hold on to everything that comes their way. Controlling people and things becomes a form of security for them…as if to try to make up the difference for their loss.

- Finding security in things - even of no value

My-sanders find security in accumulating things. The accumulation of things creates a greater sense of personal value. One of the identifiers of poor self-esteem is accumulating things as a way to increase self-worth. A My-sander's mentality tells them that *things* make them better than – and more important than – other people. Conversely, *not* accumulating things represents a loss and a decrease in self-worth and image. My-sanders pout, have pity parties, and exhibit childish behavior because they have never truly matured and are emotionally underdeveloped. When children don't get their way and put up a fuss, many times a loving parent will distract them with some other reward or thing. As the child gets older and doesn't get their way, they look to other things to make them happy. My-sanders are still in the same dynamic emotionally. They look to things to bring them comfort…like people, food, gadgets, money, and job positions, to name a few. All of these things help to give a My-sander a sense of increased self-worth. *When you are insecure in who you are, then you need things to validate you.*

[2]There is an old tale of a farmer's land which brought forth a bountiful harvest, and he had to decide how to distribute it. He spent some time deliberating and then decided to tear down his barns and build bigger ones so that he could store all of the harvest he received. He envisioned that he would be able to take it easy and relax because he had so much in the barns. What he did not know was that he would meet his death that very night. He never even had a chance to enjoy any of his harvest.

This is a clear picture of a My-sander. He had an abundance given to him and he decided to hoard it, to keep it all. His focus was only on himself and what he would get out of having so much. It probably never entered into his thinking that he could help feed some of the hungry people around his village or other surrounding areas. All he could see was himself and his needs. Who knows, perhaps if his attention were not on himself he could have enjoyed his harvest and shared some with others.

The farmer displayed the character trait of covetousness. [1]Covetousness is defined as an inordinate or wrongful desire for wealth or possessions and being greedy, especially without due regard for the rights of others. While the act of giving releases others to give to you, when you hold onto things, not only have you developed the wrong relationship with things but those things now have you! Note: We should enjoy having things, but never let things have us.

- Afraid of loss – Hoarding

The "My-sander" personality trait of holding onto things and accumulation – left unchecked – can develop into a hoarder's mentality and accompanying actions. Hoarders find comfort in the excessive collection of things. The more things that they can collect the more secure they tend to feel.

As previously stated, when someone is unbalanced in one area, this usually leads them to over-compensate in other areas. This is the characterization of hoarding; trying to get a hoarder to give up something they see that you have a need for is difficult. They will not be willing to part with anything even if it can help you. Their mindset is that they may need it sometime in the future and they cannot take the chance of giving it away. Giving something away decreases the sense of security. Until the unresolved issues (poor self-image and self-esteem) are dealt with, this behavior cannot be truly helped. Poor self-esteem cannot be fixed with a pill. However, a pill can sedate a person so that they don't think about their lack of self-esteem, but it will not make a lasting change to a person's self-esteem.

- Previous hurt or abuse – mistrust of others

It is not unusual that a My-sander personality has a history of hurt or being abused (mentally, emotionally and or physically) in past relationships. Many times My-sanders seek relationships or situations that prevent them from being hurt again. A lack of trusting others is evident with this personality. This mistrust can sustain emotional bruises that can last a lifetime. Many times, after being hurt by another person, the walls go up to keep people out. The reality of life is that you will get hurt but you cannot allow your hurts to dictate the rest of your life to you. It is on trust that meaningful relationships are built and *without trust all relationships are superficial.*

Abuse or misuse can create deep and long lasting wounds. Many times the physical wounds heal over time but the person is left with the emotional scars. With most people who are hurt emotionally, the healing of their emotions does not take place because they have not forgiven the person who hurt them. In some cases, what was done was so horrific that they feel justified by holding on to anger, hatred and unforgiveness.

By holding on to these debilitating emotions, we allow ourselves to be held captive behind the very walls that we have set into place for protection. My-sanders can be people who carry a lot of hurt, anger, pain, and unforgiveness. They have allowed their current and past situations to fuel a poor self-image and a cycle of mistrust, pain and hurt. *Hurting people can easily hurt others.* A person can only give what they possess. Too often My-sanders want to love, but have stored anger, hate, pain and unforgiveness. This is what they give out; unknowingly and habitually. Intimacy is extremely difficult, since it requires transparency and trust. So, relationships don't last because they can't give out of something that is not there. When others who they have pushed away leave the relationship, the My-sanders become even more mistrusting of people. Therefore they repeat the cycle of not trusting others, and living a life that is defensive and filled with rejection and resentment.

- Having a relationship with a My-Sander

The My-sander and My-sander personality are not "bad." Their expression and behavior are sometimes the result of complex emotional and social factors. It is important to understand that the My-sander has put up emotional barriers for protection and it will take work to get to a place of balance. They are not incapable of showing kindness, but there is a core of selfishness that has to be dealt with. One of the ways to break selfishness is to *intentionally* focus on helping other people. A good way to do this is to look for ways to reach out and help those who are less fortunate. This practice takes the attention off of self and position and puts it on someone else who really can use the help. The more practice the My-sander has with becoming involved with others and their needs, the less selfish they will become.

Being in a relationship with a My-sander can be very difficult because you will often go without having your own needs met. It is all about the My-sander and their needs. They will often be very possessive of you. They will more than likely want to control your friends, what you do and where you go. Again, if you do not have a strong sense of self, you will most likely feel used in the relationship. When your needs are met, be prepared for the My-sander to have an ulterior motive of having their needs met. They have allowed selfishness to dominate their thinking and actions. Their walls of protection will make your job of getting them to trust you very hard. This will require a lot of commitment and patience on your part.

Strengths and Weaknesses of a My-Sander Personality

Strengths: Focused, Goal-Oriented, Leadership Skills, Competent

Weaknesses: Selfish, Possessive, Lacks Emotional Intimacy, Manipulative.

Chapter Eight

The Share-Sander

Character is something that is stamped on the inside and shows on the outside.

"Share the Sand" Personality

Miriam skips ahead of her Dad, excited about getting to the playground again today to play in the sandbox. Today she is the first person to arrive at the sandbox and she can't wait for the other children to come and join her. Her Dad looks on as she plays in the sand and thinks to himself, how cool it is that she can have the sandbox all to herself and not have to deal with any of the other children. But Miriam can't wait for the other children to show up, because she loves being around others and building things with them. She sees that all of the sand is there and she could play with it all by herself, but she prefers to have others that she can build things with. She is happy to build and work on things on her own but she gets more joy out of working with others in spite some of their difficult personalities. She sees this as a challenge and a chance to help others see the good that is in them.

•Giver, helper, relationship builder

The Share-Sander personality is willing to give. They realize that giving is "where it's at." Share-Sanders know that when they give it feels as if they are in complete alignment with their true nature. They also understand that there are principles to giving that cause them to have more. They know that the more they give the more they are going to get. However, this is not the reason they give, nor is this their motivation. Share-Sanders give because they feel complete when they give and help others and it is the right thing to do.

A Share-Sander's motivation is the desire to help. They try to make bad situations good and good situations excellent. They often go the extra mile to make things the best that they can possibly be. They love giving their time, money and resources to help others. Even when it seems that they are taken advantage of (having no return on an investment) a true Share-Sander realizes that nothing that they gave or did was in vain and that there will be some good that comes out of it. True Share-Sanders are not looking to get compensated from you for their efforts. They really and truly have a heart to help and are genuine people. Living in a society where distrust exists, we can become suspicious of Share-Sanders and believe that there must be an ulterior motive behind their desire to help. They just want to give whatever is necessary to accomplish a task or to take care of a need.

Those who are willing to lend a hand will prove their loyalty to you. Likewise, those who are proverbial wolves in sheep's clothing will reveal to you who they really are, if they are around you long enough. *Character is something that is stamped on the inside and shows on the outside.* When people put on pretenses and there is no character on the inside, they can only pretend for so long before that stamp on the inside shows itself.

Share-Sanders are committed to the cause and they want to help others achieve success. They often put themselves in other people's situations and think about what they would like if they were a recipient of that help. They have a wonderful ability to empathize and sympathize with others. It is because of their ability to do this that they are extremely thoughtful people. They intentionally practice thinking about others and how they can be helpful to someone else's situation.

Share-Sanders believe the best of everyone. They are patient, kind and trustworthy and attract others to them because of these character traits. It is quite easy for Share-Sanders to build relationships with friends and with others. People are automatically attracted to someone who is stable and grounded, so the Share-Sander is easily accepted among others – in most cases. Share-Sanders are also usually excellent facilitators (because they are able to focus on the best outcome in the mix of multiple personality types.)

When a Share-Sander meets some of the other personalities that we have discussed, the other "sanders" will experience an initial attraction. However, what is taking place internally with the other "sanders" determines their continued response. When people are unbalanced and come across someone who is well-balanced, they will usually act out (show their unbalanced traits.) They only act out because of insecurities and jealousies. However, as odd as it seems – in spite of the reason for their acting out, there is a part of them that will be drawn to the person who is balanced.

•Not afraid of rejection

The Share-Sander is brave and courageous. They give even though they may not be well received and perhaps misunderstood. The satisfaction of giving and helping others far exceeds the fear of hurt and rejection. The Share-Sander realizes that life contains ups-and-downs, hurts and pain. They just refuse to compromise who they are because of a fear of being rejected. They understand that life is about giving your all and not giving excuses.

A wise man once said, [2]unless a seed falls into the ground and dies, it will never live. It is only when a seed is put into the earth that it can germinate, grow and achieve its full potential. Share-Sanders want to live their full potential out while they can. They also want to see others do the same thing. It is this drive and determination that causes them to thrive in the midst of adversity and pressures. When you help someone else succeed, you can't help but succeed! It is their relentless drive to make a difference, not just now, but in future generations. They understand that this can only be done when they take their rightful positions as Share-Sanders. They want to live life to the fullest and to die empty, instead of filled with potential.

- **Creative and optimistic thinkers**

Share-Sanders are usually very creative thinkers. Creative thinking is something that we all possess, but not everyone uses. Share-Sanders practice thinking about ways to help other people and they tend to be very optimistic, as well as creative. The average person follows a routine and does not deviate from that routine of action or thought. However, Share-Sanders are creative, and this can make routine thinkers uncomfortable. Share-Sanders have trained themselves to think creatively so when they encounter a process, they automatically look for ways to improve it. This usually irritates routine thinkers. People who have routine thinking do not see the sense in changing things. They just adapt to the norm, or status quo. They don't see the sense in making something that works 'okay' work any better. Although Share-Sanders usually are not prohibited by the routine thinker's comments or their reservations, they sometimes have to remove themselves (mentally and sometimes physically) to keep their creative juices flowing!

Optimism runs side by side with creativity for a Share-Sander, who makes the choice not to hear what cannot be done and instead chooses to think of ways to accomplish tasks and realize goals. Often, they will enlist the assistance of others to help them figure out how to accomplish what others see as impossible. Share-Sanders live in a place where their only limitations are the limits that they put on themselves. The Wright brothers are a perfect example of Share-Sanders. They believed that there was a way to fly in a machine, when all others around them laughed and scorned. Yet, something on the inside of them told them that *this could be done*. They decided to give themselves and their theory of flight as a gift to mankind. They allowed their optimism and creativity to flow and to do something that was seen as impossible at the time. Something that even today, is still quite remarkable! When we are "Share-Sanders," we receive much more than we give! When we are positive, we get positive results. Having optimism in the face of negativity and adversity is a key ingredient and partner in being creative and in having successful outcomes.

•Networks well with others

Share-Sanders are great networkers who genuinely look forward to meeting others. Many of the networking events that take place today do not reflect true networking. Regrettably, many of these events are made up of likeminded individuals trying to get what benefits them, from the event and the people who they meet. A Share-Sander may attend this event to help the people they meet; not just to have their needs met. In a networking environment, they seek to not only find individuals with whom they can connect, but they look to give what they have to others who may need it. What makes them great social networkers is that they have mastered the skill of listening. They are excellent listeners and can often repeat verbatim what you said during a conversation.

Share-Sanders are quite social and will enjoy being around others in social settings. They are usually very pleasant people to be around, because they are genuinely interested in your welfare. Share-Sanders like to know how the family is doing and all of the other day-to-day things that are happening in someone else's life. Someone who possesses these traits makes it very easy to talk to and get to know on better terms. It is this type of person that we look to form lasting bonds with. They make you feel appreciated and they value you as a person (your thoughts and ideas.) This is not something that can be mimicked. It has to be genuine. Truth recognizes Truth!

- Maximizes the power of "Team"

Share-Sanders know and realize that they need others in order to truly succeed. Success is never accomplished in a vacuum. They understand that it often takes a team to really accomplish something of significance. They know that they can only do so much by themselves, but with a team they can accomplish so much more. Share-Sanders want to reach as far as they can and help as many as they can. They maximize the power of 'team' as much as possible. They count the successes of others as their success.

- Develops the Team

A strong team is effective in that its reach is broader and the potential work accomplished is greater than what one individual can do. Frequently, a leader has to work with a team that they have not chosen, and is assigned to achieve specific goals by an organization. What makes the Share-Sander unique as a Team leader/Manager/Director/VP, or CEO is the fact that they care for their team and want to help and develop them on a personal, as well as a professional level. They see the potential and ability in every team member. No matter what the objective or task, the Share-Sander focuses on the goal <u>and</u> the welfare of the team. Therefore, a Share-Sander like Miriam, can work with:

Harry – who takes the sand;
Robert – who eats the sand;
Big Mike – who crushes what you are building in the sand;
Johnny – who poops in the sand;
Laura – who throws the sand;
Jacob – who complains about the sand;
Janice – who does not share the sand.

Miriam knows how to make the best out of relating and working with each of them. This is accomplished by not judging these individuals and personalities or focusing on their weaknesses, but by getting them to see and build upon their strengths *while* managing their weaknesses. A Share-Sander (aka The Sharer) will teach these individuals not to ignore their weaknesses but to manage them.

Life principle: What we focus on will be magnified and what we magnify will be fixed in our sight. When we focus on our weaknesses, we make them bigger and stronger in our lives. Consequently, when we look at weaknesses we will act, look and feel weak. Likewise, when we focus on our strengths we will act, look and feel strong.

•Personality Encounters

Miriam is now all grown up and so are the other toddlers in the box. As she moves through life (the big sandbox) she comes across many of the toddlers/adults that we have discussed. As you can imagine not much has changed since the sandbox days, but Miriam is a leader and knows how to work with and develop those around her. The following are her relationship interactions and influences that she has with each personality:

•The Taker

Miriam will first have a conversation with Harry (aka the Taker) where she will share with him that he is a natural leader because of his drive, determination and laser focus. She will, most importantly, listen to him without judging him. Then she will begin to tell him what remarkable things he has accomplished and the great potential that she sees in him. She will also explain to him the *potential* blockers that are holding him back from being the stronger leader that he desires to become. She will mentor him by showing him:

a) How to give (serve) and shift his focus off of taking. As he begins to give he will experience a level of satisfaction that he had not experienced before. This will help in taking his focus from himself and being a taker.

b) How to use his persistence positively for the benefit of the team. He will learn that he can be assertive and not overly aggressive like in his past. He will see Miriam's strong communications skills in action when Miriam is having interactions with the team and other stake holders.

c) How following authority and exercising self-control ultimately makes him a stronger person. He will see that there are benefits to following the rules and guidelines and how they can help him accomplish his goals, both personally and professionally. He will learn that self-control is the highest form of control that one can achieve. Once he is balanced in this area he will become happier person.

d) Harry will learn that leaders <u>take responsibility</u> for their actions. Miriam will model this behavior to help him realize that *his real wealth lies within his character*....

•The Eater

Miriam will show Robert (aka the Eater) that greatness is on the inside of him, and share how to live genuinely (free from pretense) and not be afraid of who he is. She will point him in the direction of self-discovery. *Self-discovery is the Eater's key to success*. Robert's gifts and talents – many of which he may not even be aware of – will be pointed out by Miriam. She will show Robert how to operate with efficiency while being productive with their efforts when carrying out a task. This will model to Robert the importance of prioritizing and not procrastinating or waiting to the last moment to get things done. Robert will see that fully focusing on the right thing will leave no room for him to focus on the wrong thing, or better yet "no"-thing. This will encourage and inspire Robert to live life with intent and meaning. This will cause Robert to become the bright star that he was meant to be.

•The Crusher

Miriam will demonstrate to Mike (aka the Crusher) how not to be discouraged by the success of others and how to use their success in a positive way to fuel his dreams. She explains to Mike that if someone else is obtaining their dreams, he should not feel jealous or envious but know that he can reach his dreams, also. Miriam will teach Mike how to not give up on his dreams and not quit. She will show through experience that persistence has its rewards and that quitting is not an option. She displays to Mike an uncanny ability to focus on the prize and not on the distractions in life that can hold him back. Miriam reveals to Mike that *his answer to his frustration lies in building and not crushing.* Because Miriam loves herself, this positive self-image and genuine love for others will show Mike that being negative, hating and crushing is not the answer. Lastly, Mike will see how to funnel the negative energy used for crushing, to build something of significance. This significance is not what is important to others, but what is important to him. Once Mike builds what is of significance to him then he will be fulfilled, live with resolve and accomplish great things.

•The Pooper

Miriam will show Johnny (aka the Pooper) how to face fear head on and to come out of his shell of insecurity. She will display confidence even when they are in situations that they have not been in before. This will let Johnny know that when life throws him a curve ball, he can still hit a home run. It also shows him that it is equally, if not *more important, to have the right attitude…not necessarily the right answer.* Johnny will see that it is having the right attitude that will lead him to the right answer, when things don't go as planned. Miriam will remain calm and collective during the upsets of the day, without panicking and making rash decisions. Johnny will learn to respond to problems rather than reacting to them. Without taking on the title of "Coach," Miriam will show Johnny how to be his best. Johnny will see the value of having a coach to help him along the way.

•The Thrower

Miriam assesses Laura's (aka the Thrower) current situation and sees that she is really hurting on the inside. She empathizes with her situation of not really feeling like she belongs. She understands that Laura often feels like a square peg trying to fit into a round hole. She gets Laura's frustration which gets Laura's attention which is not usually easy. It is because she understands and feels Laura's pain that Laura feels safe around her, and is willing to let go of the drama, in hope of an answer to the agony of her soul. Instead of Laura getting an answer from Miriam, she is met with the questions that she has avoided for so long. Miriam will help Laura seek the answers to the questions that have caused her frustrations such as: Why am I here? What am I supposed to do? Where am I going? Miriam realizes that if Laura does not take the time out of life's busyness (drama) to answer these questions, she is doomed to a life of frustration, pain and resentment. Laura becomes cognizant of the fact that *these answers are the keys to her life and to her living in the fullness of who she was created to be.* It is the direct result of her true introspection that will bring about the true answers that will cause Laura to believe in herself. This will put Laura on the right path to her destiny.

•The Complainer

Miriam's leadership will show Jacob (aka the Complainer) how not to fall apart when expectations are met with disappointment. Also how he can rework the plan so that new expectations can be met. This teaches Jacob how to move forward and not get stuck in the mistakes and failures of the past. Miriam will share with Jacob her expertise in how to view the people and situations in his life positively. Jacob will see that Miriam chooses, purposely, to see the good and positive even when things look dim. This will cause Jacob to push pass past limitations and surge forward to new opportunities while keeping an optimistic attitude. Most importantly, Miriam will show him how his words are a creative force. She will explain to Jacob that his words (spoken thoughts) have great power whether used negatively or positively. Jacob has a new understanding about words and the weight that they carry. He realizes that his words carry a certain power behind them and when they are released they set a positive or negative atmosphere. *He now uses favorable words to create a climate where both he and things can grow*. This allows him to work in an environment where he can now be creative and build without casting the blame and finger pointing. He becomes accountable for his thought life, words and actions.

•The My-Sander

Miriam will teach Janice (aka the My-Sander) that her desire for control is best used within, as self-control. She will show Janice how to control her emotions, deal with discouragement, and balance having fun while still being responsible for her actions. Miriam's lifestyle preaches before she even opens her mouth. Her integrity, passion, inspiration, positive attitude, calm demeanor, and visionary leadership speaks louder than her words could ever speak. Miriam will show Janice that it is truly more blessed to give than to hold on. Miriam gives her time, resources, expertise and wisdom to others and this causes exponential growth in her life. When she gives, it is given back to her many times over. Janice sees the love in the relationships, the joy that's received from giving, and the mark that is made on the recipients of the effort and time given to them by Miriam. She perceives the contrast of Miriam's life versus hers. Janice has been hurt and still is not sure that she can learn to trust others, but what she sees creates a desire for change. Miriam explains to her that in life people can and probably will disappoint/hurt her but it is up to her to walk in forgiveness, love and *integrity*. She encourages her to stop hiding herself under these walls of negativity and adversity (hurt, pain, unforgiveness). As long as she hides behind the pain, hurt and mistrust of the past she cannot be her true self. Miriam shares with Janice that *integrity is what will allow her to be true to self.* It is the truth to self that will allow her to be true to others. Miriam further explains that, *it is through truth that she will become authentic and her true identity will be found.* Once Janice's identity is found, she will not have her security wrapped up in things, but in who she has become.

- Share-Sanders Inspire

It is by Miriam's positive influence that her interactions with the other sandbox personalities are constructive and productive. She knows her purpose in life. Therefore, she lives on purpose. Her character speaks for itself and she is strong, powerful and a confident leader. While Miriam is not the savior of the world (perfect) she understands that she can only show the way. She cannot make people change. However, she inspires others by her actions and lifestyle to follow and pursue their dreams and aspirations. A true leader she is, and as a true "sharer" she gives (serves).

- The Ideal Sharer

Ants are the ideal "sharers" of the insect kingdom and we can learn a lot when we evaluate an ant colony. By looking at how they work together we get a glimpse perhaps at how relationships in life could or should be. It is a great testimony of how, when we work together great things can be accomplished both in our relationships and the marketplace.

A Picture Inside of the Ant Kingdom

1) The first thing that we notice about the ants is that they work tirelessly in their activities. Perhaps this is due to the fact that *everything that they do is tied to a specific purpose.*

2) The ants are *goal-oriented*. They store food in large quantities. This shows that the ants not only have a purpose for their activities but that they have goals as well.

3) The ants *create* tunnels underground that allow air to circulate through the soil. This is *foresight*. The ants foresee the need ahead of time and put a system in place to take care of that need before it arises.

4) Ants are *strong* and can lift 50 times their body weight. Ants *focus on their strength* and not their size or what the other bigger insects might think about them. Their focus is not on how others might view them, or their perceived weaknesses.

5) Ants have a great sense of smell. This means that they are actively *seeking out opportunities*. Although it may appear to others that they are wandering or walking in circles they are not bothered by the fact that they have not found food yet (failure). They continue in the hunt knowing, if they *don't give up* but keep looking, they will succeed in finding a food source (success).

6) Ants are *highly social* and *highly organized*. They *build community*, depend on each other and understand that they are all in this together. They know that they stand a better chance of survival if they *work together*. They also know that they cannot work together without order.

7) Ants *share* their food with others. When an ant finds a food source, they don't sit there and eat and say, "Every ant for themselves," but they carry the food back to the nest for the entire colony. They also tell the other ants where the source is located. They don't hoard the prize. They share.

What we learn from observing the ant colony is fascinating. They put in practice these simple principles that – if we followed them – would create great success for us, our families and our societies. This is the power of working as a unified team!

- Staying on course

When you open yourself up to helping people, you automatically open yourself up to hurt and disappointments because people are unpredictable. However, you should not be discouraged. Be encouraged because you can make a difference. Have the courage to be true to who you are. Don't get conformed to the hurts and pains that you may experience in life. It takes real power to stand true to who you were created to be. Remember, it is those Share-Sanders with courage and perseverance whom we now call heroes (e.g., Gandhi, Mandela, Martin Luther King, Jr., Mother Teresa, and the like).

Strengths and Weaknesses of a Sharer Personality

Strengths: Leader, Giver, Sees the Best in people, Develops others, Visionary, Creative, Purposeful, Positive, Social, Highly Organized, Achiever, and Instinctive.

Weaknesses: Too trusting at times. Can be taken advantage of.

Chapter Nine

Driving Factors

When you can love and treat yourself with value, you will begin to attract those that treat you the same way.

There are many things that can be attributed to a person's behaviors. The sandbox shows us just how some of these behaviors are formed and acted out. In this chapter I would like to look at two intrinsic forces that drive the unwanted behavior in the sandbox. These two forces can create havoc in a relationship. In most cases the individuals in the relationship don't realize that they are present. When we can identify the problem it greatly increases our chances of being able to resolve the problem with a solution. The two main forces are *rejection* and *insecurity*. Both forces are invisible and work in harmony to create a myriad of visible chaos. They cause strife, division, divorce, arguments and turmoil, in countless ways. Let's take a look at these two enemies of relationships, rejection first followed by insecurity.

- Rejection

To [1]reject means to refuse to accept, acknowledge or believe; to throw out as useless, worthless; to discard. Rejection is what happens to us when we have had and interaction or experience in which we perceive that our ideas, thoughts, beliefs and our person have been disregarded.

Value is something that we all have for ourselves. If we were to take two individuals on both spectrums of the value scale (high and low), we would see that we all set some type of value on ourselves. Whether we register low on the scale or high, we still value ourselves and we do not like our value to be taken away by someone else. When we feel like we are not honored (valued) it is easy to feel rejected.

As individuals we are married to our most dominant thoughts and in most cases it is difficult to separate ourselves from our thoughts and ideas. So when someone has ideas and thoughts about a particular subject and their ideas are rejected they can feel useless and worthless. Because a person and their dominant thoughts are one, when our ideas are rejected we feel rejected. We feel like our value has been chipped at once again. These feelings of rejection cause scars emotionally and we bleed emotionally (internally) but it is not seen physically. Rejection can cause pain in our souls and if it is not dealt with correctly we will began to infect others with the same pain in an attempt to bandage our own hurt.

- Some other ways we can feel or be rejected

    1) Character is something that we all possess, good or bad. However, when our character is attacked we get defensive and go into protection mode. Even someone who lacks good character does not appreciate when someone talks about their character. *Character assassination* leads us to feel rejected.

    2) Being *ignored or overlooked* can leave us with this feeling of rejection. When someone is ignored (intentionally or unintentionally) the message that is being sent to them is that you do not matter. Ignoring sends the idea that someone doesn't exist. Everyone has a sense of significance and when someone refrains from noticing or recognizing them, this can create long lasting emotional wounds (hurt).

3) When others don't want us around and decide to let us know how they really feel about our presence, it's what I call blunt force rejection (BFR). BFR is what many children deal with every day in a form of *bullying*. Bullies look for individuals that they can push around through physical force or intimidation. When a person feels like their rights have been stripped from them and they cannot be their authentic selves, they will either:
 a) push-back, b) try to be someone else, or 3) stay true to themselves while they deal with the pain of being bullied and rejected.

4) When people tell us *NO* or, to *STOP,* it can lead to feelings of rejection. I am in no way suggesting that every time we hear those words that we are dealing with rejection. What I am saying is when we really have our hearts set to do something, and then we hear those words, it can *feel like* rejection. When we are in a relationship with someone these are often the words that can hurt the most. Just as we can feel rejected when our ideas and thoughts are rejected, we often feel the same way when our actions are rejected with the words no and/or stop.

5) Not being accepted or a *lack of reassurance* from others fosters an atmosphere for rejection. Sometimes this can be because we are different from others (we think, look and act differently). We all on some level seek to be accepted. This is just how we are wired from the factory. As independent as we may be we still depend on each other for social connections. The more meaningful the relationship connection the more reassurance we

need. We need to know that we are acceptable to the people that we love and admire. In many marriages, often one partner goes with this need being unmet. In working relationships we often seek the approval of those that we are working for. Whether it is because we did a great job on the project or are just looking to be appreciated. When we don't feel *appreciated* we can feel rejected. However, we must be careful that we don't become unbalanced and need constant reassurance and approval from others. This often leads to insecurity, which we will cover next.

The bottom line is that being rejected hurts. Rejection feels like you have been punched, hit, or battered by someone's words and/or actions, or from your own perceived thoughts. There have been several experiments done on social rejection and they have shown that *the same part of the brain that registers physical pain is the same part of the brain that registers emotional pain.* This may explain why medication is prescribed for emotional problems. Some psychologist believe that when someone has experienced social rejection, they either lash out at the ones responsible for the rejection or they seek a group or place where they are accepted. The problem is, when the person lashes out at others, this pushes them further away from being accepted by the group. This almost always sets the individual up for another bout of rejection from the same group. When the individual does not lash out, but finds a group or person that accepts them, they become more emotionally balanced. Rejection can be toxic. An emotionally healthy person understands that rejection will happen. They also understand that they cannot allow rejection to determine their internal image or outcome. While we can't stop rejection from happening we can determine how we will deal with it when it happens. We should never allow rejection or a person's opinion to define us. If we are different and don't quite fit in…that is okay. I often refer to this quote about rejection, *"Some people are going to reject you, simply because you smile too bright for them. And that's okay. Keep smiling!"* [3]Author unknown

- Insecurity

[1]Insecurity means subject to fears, doubt; not confident or assured: not tightly fastened. Many times the root cause of insecurity is abuse, abandonment and rejection. We can also have insecurities about the way we look (body shape, height, weight, and skin color) achievements and educational levels.

When we are insecure we are unbalanced. In an attempt to balance ourselves out we can become increasing attached to people, behaviors and things in an unhealthy way. We can form unhealthy relationships with material things and become possessive of those we are in relationships with. These behaviors are intrinsically motivated and are triggered any time the person feels insecure. There are certain situations that can cause a person to feel insecure. At these times their routine behavior will be modeled, therefore making the person with the insecurity predictable.

- Insecurity from Abandonment

Insecurity in a relationship can translate to a smothering type behavior, especially if the insecurity is fed from abandonment. If someone has a fear of being left alone, they can become possessive of the other person's time in their relationship. They may want to control all of their free time to make sure that it is being spent with them. It is natural to want to spend time with those that they love and have a relationship with. It is when they feel like they need to have that person around them all of the time that this behavior can be unhealthy.

Abandonment issues can be severe, or subtle. A severe case may be that a mother/father left their family for another family, or because of a drug addiction. Or perhaps a baby was put up for adoption and the child grew up with a loving family that cared for them and treated them as their own. However, as the child becomes older and knows that they are adopted they begin to develop an abandonment wound, wondering why their biological family has left them. A more subtle approach might be a woman who just went through a break-up with her longtime lover, who she thought would someday be her husband. Perhaps her lover has moved on to someone else and she is now wondering if she is not good enough, "Why did they leave?" In either case the wound is the same type…whether one went deep or just scratched the surface. The wound says, "Why did they leave me?"

It is often from this internal question that insecurity from abandonment is birthed. This can cause the person with an abandonment issue to become smothering in their relationships. They will also try to do whatever it takes to keep the person in the relationship. They will often put up with things that they do not like and people that they do not like, just to keep the relationship together. The relationship is no longer driven by love, but by need. *A relationship driven by need, instead of love, will always be in turmoil.* The reason for this is because anytime the need goes unmet the individual will become unbalanced and begin to act out by showing unpleasant behavior that threatens the stability of the relationship.

For instance, Jerry and Katy have been dating now for six months. Jerry is very smothering and wants to spend all of his free time with Katy. Jerry has plans to spend this weekend with Katy watching movies and just hanging together like they do most weekends. Katy decides that she wants to hang out with her girlfriends for a girls' night out on Saturday. Katy shares her plans with Jerry on Thursday, over the phone while she is at work, and explains that she just wants to be with her girlfriends. The mere suggestion that Katy wants to do something without Jerry sends Jerry into a twister of emotions. He becomes fearful that she will like being away from him and doing things without him more often. Jerry is jealous that Katy might find someone better and leave. Jerry thinks this way because this is what happened in his last relationship. Jerry is also dealing with the fact that when he was eight years old, his mother left him and his dad for another man. Jerry becomes furious with Katy and she has no idea why this is such a big deal. She does not understand Jerry's anger. After a not-so-pleasant exchange of heated emotions by both parties, Katy decides it is not worth it. She decides to stay home on Saturday with Jerry and watch movies, but she is resentful the entire time.

Jerry smothers because of a fear of being alone. Whenever his need to feel wanted is threatened, he becomes angry and irrational. It is this behavior that makes Katy crave for space in their relationship; the very thing that Jerry fears most. He is blind to the fact that it is *his* behavior that is creating a separation in his relationships.

- Insecurity fed from rejection

Insecurity can cause us to underrate ourselves through what we say internally about ourselves, especially in cases where the insecurity is fed from rejection. As we covered earlier, rejection hurts. Our value comes from the picture that we see of ourselves. It is how we interpret how we look to others based on what we see when we look internally. *How we see ourselves determines the internal conversation that we have with ourselves.* When our internal conversation is negative it is because we are seeing ourselves as a minus and not a plus. When we see ourselves that way we think we are undeserving and our words follow what we see and say internally. It is very hard to see the good because we are looking intrinsically at the negative. Our true words always follow our most dominate thoughts and images. This image is what contributes to our self-esteem. If the image is looked at in a negative way we will have poor self-esteem. Likewise, if our image of ourselves is healthy and positive, we will have healthy self-esteem.

In the story above, Jerry faced abandonment issues but he also felt rejected because his mother left him. Even though his mother had her own set of issues, Jerry sees it as he is not good enough. He believes that "something is wrong with him" and "If everything was okay with him then his mother would have never left." He feels that Katy is going to leave him also because he is not the full package. Secretly, he has a hole within that he tries to mask with an external solution (smothering). His self-image is damaged which has contributed to his lack of self-confidence. An external solution will only be a bandage on an internal wound. What Jerry does not realize is that his value does not come from what his mother did or did not do. Neither does it come from his relationship with Katy. Jerry's value must come from a new self-image.

A healthy self-image feeds self-confidence. In other words, when Jerry's internal picture of self has value and is positive, Jerry's self-confidence will increase. Jerry can also start to make positive affirmations to himself. His words will begin to paint a picture in his imagination. When Jerry tells himself that he has great value and worth, his imagination goes to work to change his negative internal picture of himself. Many people try this a few times and give up. Then they say that this does not work. What many miss is the fact that they have been internally talking negativity to themselves, for years. They want to tell themselves something positive ten times and have instant results. This will not work. The old foundation (negative framework) has to be dug up and new words and images need to be planted to hold the new framed picture in the imagination.

Self-confidence can also be built by making good decisions. When Jerry starts making better decisions he will have better outcomes. Having better outcomes automatically boosts his self-confidence. *Confidence builds courage.* When Jerry finds confidence he can then have the courage to trust himself. Trusting himself has been what he has secretly been seeking after. It is when he can trust himself that he will find his true value. Trusting himself allows him to trust others. When he can trust others he will not need to be smothering because he will have a sense of security from within. Then Jerry will not allow Katy's (or anyone else's) actions or behavior to define his worth or dictate his behavior.

- Insecurity birthed from abuse breeds distrust

Insecurity can breed distrust of others and those you are in a relationship with, especially, if the insecurity was birthed from abuse. When abuse has taken place it leaves a deep emotional wound that shows up in a person as distrust toward almost everyone. All abuse is painful to live through no matter what the situation. However, those who were abused by those who were close to them seem to suffer the most damage. They wonder, "How could someone who is supposed to love me do this to me or stand by while the abuse took place." They believe that if they can't trust those who were supposed to protect them, then how can they feel safe around others? They begin to create invisible barriers that won't allow people to get to close to them. These barriers are a form of self-defense to protect them because they have lost trust in those around them. They walk through life holding people and friends at a distance in an attempt to protect themselves from being hurt again.

Remember, the person who does not let others in cannot let themselves out. The person who has been abused has every right to keep themselves in, but their *rights* are making a big *wrong* in their life. You cannot live your life to the fullest by being in fear of being hurt. Your bad experiences are not who you are and you should not let them define you. Forgiveness is the key. Forgiveness is not just for the person that hurt you but it is more for you. When you release someone else, it releases you! When you can trust yourself to forgive and move on, you will begin to trust others that you are in relationships with. Trust is not built in a day. You don't want to just trust everyone with everything. Trust has to be earned and built over time. However you want to have the ability to trust and allow others in, as opposed to keeping everyone out.

Picture yourself standing in front of a door. The door opens and you see something you really desire on the other side of the doorway. You notice that you have a large suitcase in your hands that will not make it through the narrow doorway. You come to terms that you will have to leave the suitcase in order to get through the door and to what you desire. The suitcase is your unforgiveness. Unforgiveness allows you to keep emotional baggage that you no longer need. Forgiveness allows you to move on in life. Don't stay in the doorway and hold on to the baggage of unforgiveness. Your worth is too great not to share your gifts and talents with the world. Don't let your baggage keep you in your past. Let it go and move forward with your life.

- **Dealing with insecurities about the way we look, our educational levels and achievements**

Many times we can have insecurities that are based on our outer appearance, educational levels and lack of success. Having these types of insecurities are damaging as well because they tell us we are not good enough. These types of feelings can cause us to self loathe and live in an unhealthy emotional state. When we carry self-hatred we will begin to carry self-sabotaging habits that support our dislike for ourselves. This negative thinking begins to create a circuit or cycle of negativity that for some can be never-ending.

A [1]circuit is defined as: *a circular journey or one beginning and ending at the same place; a round.* Thoughts create or complete a circuit in the mind. As a particular thought rolls in our minds over and over it begins to gain strength and momentum to the point where it makes us act. Once we act, the thought begins again with more strength and repeats this cycle all over again. The only way to break this cycle is to inject another thought into the mind that will replace the previous thought.

When a negative thought of insecurity starts on its journey to complete its circuit it picks up 'friends' along the way that think the same way. Some of its 'friends' are uncertainty, self-doubt, hesitancy, and indecision. These thoughts create a habitation for action that leads to self-sabotage (bad behavior). Unless a positive thought is interjected repeatedly into the mind to break the negative thought pattern from completing its cycle, the person will remain in a same state of mind and feel trapped. Therefore they will continue in the same behavior.

To break out of the prison of negative thinking and behavior, new positive thoughts will need to be introduced. Your mind cannot hold a positive and negative thought at the same time. Knowing this, you will have to catch yourself when you begin to think negatively. Once you notice that you are not thinking correctly you will have to intentionally think positively about yourself. This will begin the eviction process of insecurity. Insecurity will have no choice but to leave when you start to think about yourself in a positive way.

You will also have to begin to love yourself. I know that this may sound funny but part of the reason that you may be carrying insecurity is because you do not completely love you. *When you don't love yourself, you will not be able to truly accept another person's love.* I am not saying that you cannot find anyone to love you. I am saying you will not be able to truly receive their love because you will need to love yourself first. When you can love yourself, then you can give love and receive love appropriately. When you have insecurities that say, "I don't love/like myself" (negative picture of self) you will not have the capacity to receive that someone can truly love you (because you don't like or love yourself). When this is the case and someone is trying to love someone that does not love themselves, the person who is not capable of receiving love will allow self-sabotaging behavior to surface, which many times pushes the other person away.

Often when someone doesn't love themselves they will attract people in their relationships that will not treat them properly. It is almost like they are sending out an invisible signal that others can pick up on. For example, when you own something valuable but don't treat it well, you invite others to also not treat it well. *When you can love and treat yourself with value, you will begin to attract those that treat you the same way.*

- **Don't just feed your needs**

As long as you are focused on yourself and your needs, your relationships will be on auto-pilot to fail. Insecurity keeps your focus on your needs. In order for a relationship to be healthy and grow you will need to focus on the other people in your relationships. As I stated earlier, many times the root cause to insecurity is through abuse, abandonment and rejection. These are all things that can happen to an individual externally that leave them with an internal wound. Many times the physical abuse, abandonment and rejection only last for a short time compared to the emotional wounds that can last a lifetime. These physical acts can cause the recipient to carry within themselves an, "I am flawed" mindset. Nothing is further from the truth. You are not the sum total of your experiences and you are not the victim, but you are the victor!

Using the following exercise can help you with improving your self-image. Having a better self-image can help to evict the rejection and insecurity scars that have been plaguing you. Your outcome should be that you have a better value and view of yourself.

Improving Self-image
Exercise

1) Write down ten ways you would like to see yourself in a more positive way: (e.g., strong, healthy, wealthy, confident, etc.). Post the list on your bathroom mirror so you can see it every day.

2) Use a recording device to record what you wrote down (example…make affirming statements like, "I am strong," etc.)

3) Look at yourself in the mirror and say to yourself, at least three times a day, what you wrote about how you would like to see yourself.

4) Listen to yourself on the recorder before you go to sleep at night. The voice that you will believe the most will be your own. Going to sleep with it playing on repeat throughout the night will help the process.

5) Read uplifting books and articles and listen to positive music (lyrics that add life). You will need to foster an atmosphere that is positive and remove yourself from negative situations.

6) Do something very nice for yourself at least once a month (a massage, clothes shopping, a nice meal at a fancy restaurant, etc.).

7) Engage in physical exercise. The gym, jogging, or walking and a healthy diet will do wonders for your self-esteem. Note: consult your physician before starting an exercise program or new diet.

Chapter Ten

Moving Forward

A devout life learner is always looking to improve on the man he was yesterday.

There are many factors to changing and being our best. In no way do I believe that I covered all of them in this book. However, I would like to share with you these two keys that I believe will help you as you encounter the different personalities and navigate through the sandboxes of your life. These two keys are, living free from your past and winning the external fight internally. These are the two keys that we will need to practice over and over, as we will always have new opportunities to create a new past and face new internal fights as we grow and develop. Remember, *a devout life learner is always looking to improve on the man he was yesterday.*

- **Living free from your past**

Many times things may have happened to you that may have been unfair. People may have hurt you but don't allow them to keep you in an emotional prison for the rest of your life. Insecurity is in direct relationship with fear. Fear is designed to hold you back or to paralyze you. Fears leave when you face them! Don't allow your past to hold your future as a hostage. It is not too late for you to live your life free from the pains of your past. You have so much ahead of you, dreams, ambitions, goals that you must reach. *Give your past its final farewell and move forward.*

Part of moving forward is realizing what has been ailing you and being honest about it. The first person you must be honest with is yourself. You can also confide in a friend or a professional, whichever one you feel more comfortable with. You will find that by being honest with yourself and *sharing* your heart with a trustworthy friend or professional will start the healing process.

You have many gifts and talents that have been wrapped inside of you. Release all of them and keep the door to your heart open. Many of us close the door to keep others out and for protection (self-preservation.) The problem with closing the door to your heart is that what you have to offer is not able to be released in its fullness (your best).

In order to truly be free from the fear of being hurt you must keep your heart open and risk the chance that you can be hurt again. The reason you are doing this is not to be hurt again but to allow yourself to live again. This will allow you to forgive the folks that hurt you. When you live this way it causes you to truly love again without the fears and insecurities of the past. When you love this way you will love yourself in a way that you could not before. A valued, secured, confident and empowered image is what you will see when you look internally. Consequently, this is what will show when others see you as well.

- Winning the external fight internally

It is after you put your past in its place that you can begin to focus on your future. Remember, you cannot change people or your past but *you* can change *your* perspective. How you see things and internalize them is the key to your success. For this to take place you will have to develop your mind. For starters, you will need to see conflicts in life as a favorable condition for advancement. Yes, without opposition there will be no success. In order to win there must be an opponent, in order to have victory there must be a fight. Many times people fight each other with their behavior and they believe that people are the problem. However, our biggest battles take place within. *It is the fight within us that we often overlook because we become so preoccupied with other people.* The external fight with others takes our attention from the real battle that is taking place within us. The internal fight within us is the battle for our minds. Who really has control? Is it us or is it the preprogrammed response that we have to external stimuli? Our most valuable asset is our mind. It is through the well-developed, disciplined mind that we are able to change our perspective to see oppositions as opportunities (favorable conditions for advancement).

When we are around others we remember how we *felt* rather than what we were *thinking*. We later began to tie our feeling with our thoughts based on the interaction, whether it was a positive or negative. What we felt from being around someone is usually tied to the behavior and or the vibes that we felt from them. This causes us to draw a conclusion on whether we want to further connect or disassociate with this person. It can also dictate to us our behavior when we interact with them. Are we defensive (on guard) or relaxed and comfortable? Do we need to change who we are, around them? Do we treat them negatively (nasty) or nice? Is there a lot to talk about or is the conversation short and to the point? The list goes on…more and more questions arise and we come to an automatic response based on the interactions and encounters that we have with the various personalities that we come in contact with.

The best way to control our outcomes is to first, understand how we internalize and process the things that lead us to our conclusions. Second, is to recognize that we can interrupt the process and determine our own conclusion and respond to the individuals we come in contact with. *When we predetermine our response, it does not matter what challenges we face externally*. Our response to external stimuli will be to act assertively and confidently with our behavior, foreseeing a favorable outcome. This is not something that is easy, but with a lot of practice can be mastered (don't worry…life will give you plenty of tests). This is the power of a disciplined mind that can turn unfavorable instances into successful outcomes – where our actions don't have to mimic or get its cues from someone else's behavior.

Our minds dictate to us our actions and behaviors. When we can control our minds, then we can control our behavior and the way we react and respond to the various situations that we encounter. To take control of our minds and to tell ourselves positively what we are going to do and how to act (positive behavior) is one of the highest forms of control that we can possess. This is what will bring about maturity in our behavior and within our relationships.

- Which personality type am I?

While I was writing this book and sharing the concept, many of my friends asked me which personality (behavior) type I associated with. My answer was **"All of them!"** I felt like there was a little piece of me in every personality. While I may have one personality type that is more dominant, I could still see some traits of other personalities. This might be true for you as well. While one personality may be more dominant than others they all need to strive to be more like the Share-Sander. While this personality is not perfect, it provides the basis of true leadership.

When writing the Share-Sander personality, I thought mostly of my lovely wife (Lloyda). She was my inspiration behind the Share-Sander personality. She is one of the people I am most proud to say is in my sandbox. A true leader she is, and as a true Sharer – she gives.

To me, the ultimate Share-Sander of mankind is Jesus Christ. Whether you believe in Jesus as a man of history, a religious figure, or deity, His life was one of an ultimate Share-Sander. He goes down in the history and religious books as one who gave Himself for the betterment of all mankind.

May you see and release your true potential for greatness!

I wish you much success in your sandbox.

- Allen

www.AFspeaks.com

Order your Audio CD of "Releasing the Sand – discovering your true potential"

Releasing the Sand is an audio CD that will: a) inspire you to become the best you that you can be, b) teach strategies for overcoming the barriers to progress, c) help you build strong, meaningful relationships, and d) empower you with powerful leadership skills to live your life on purpose.

www.AFspeaks.com/products

Knowing who is in the Sandbox with you can make all of the difference

Personalities/Traits Quick Guide

Below is a quick guide to some notable character traits of the different personalities that we have discussed. These are just some of the traits you might encounter if you have interactions with these individuals.

TAKER	THROWER
1. ARROGANT	1. ANGRY
2. BULLY	2. BLAMEFUL
3. DISRESPECTFUL	3. COMMOTIONS & TANTRUMS
4. ENTITLED	4. FRUSTRATED
5. NARCISSISTIC	5. IMMATURE
6. OVERBEARING	6. PRONE TO DEPRESSION
7. USER	7. VENGEFUL

EATER	COMPLAINER
1. APPEARS LAZY	1. BLAMEFUL
2. DREAMER WITHOUT ACTION	2. DISAGREEABLE
3. EASILY DISTRACTED	3. EXCUSE MAKER
4. LOSES TRACK OF TIME	4. FUSSING
5. NOT MOTIVATED	5. NEGATIVE OUTLOOK
6. OVERLY ANALYTICAL	6. NEGATIVE SPEECH
7. PROCRASTINATOR	7. PRONE TO DEPRESSION

Quick Guide, continued:

POOPER
1. EASILY CONFUSED
2. FEARFUL
3. METHODICAL
4. MISINTERPRETS SOCIAL CUES
5. PANICKY
6. **POOR DECISION MAKER**

MY SANDER
1. LONER
2. NARROW-MINDED
3. OPPORTUNISTIC
4. POSSESSIVE
5. SELFISH
6. UNTRUSTING

CRUSHER
1. ANGRY
2. DISPLAYS HATRED
3. EASILY DISAPPOINTED
4. FRUSTRATED
5. HOSTILE
6. **JEALOUS**

SHARER
1. FRIENDLY
2. GIVING
3. KIND
4. LOVING
5. LOYAL
6. NURTURING

References

[1] Definition from dictionary.com

[2] Story excerpt or quote taken from the Holy Bible (emphasis added, and some changes to the storyline may have been added).

For more detailed reference info visit
www.AFspeaks.com/reference

[3] Author unknown or unable to verify author of quote

About the Author

Allen Forbes is an inspiring, powerful and exciting speaker. He is a business consultant and the well-known author of Sandbox Personalities.

Prior to co-founding Living Life International, Allen was as a successful operations and sales/marketing professional for a Fortune 500 company. He was responsible for accounts with over 100 million dollars in revenue. Allen gained the nickname, "the hitting wonder," for routinely putting together multi-million dollar deals. Allen earned the title of top sales professional multiple times during his tenure with the organization.

Allen is committed to helping others transform their lives so that they can live in their purpose and dreams. He adds a unique value to his presentations by combining biblical principles along with extensive business knowledge and wisdom. Allen is also known for his inspiring, engaging, and energetic communication style. He inspires and encourages individuals, audiences and teams to reach their personal and professional goals and to achieve individual success.

Allen has been happily married to his wife, Lloyda, for over 24 years and they are the proud guardians of two adorable and energetic children. Allen and his family reside in the USA.

Request Allen to speak at your next event

www.AFspeaks.com/request-allen

Share your sandbox stories with us

www.AFspeaks.com/sandbox-stories

Business Solutions

www.AFspeaks.com/business-solutions

Follow Allen on Facebook
www.facebook.com/allen.forbes.12

Follow Allen on Twitter
https://twitter.com/AllenForbes

Follow Allen on Google+
https://plus.google.com/u/0/b/107282113609165213895/+Afspeaks/posts

If you enjoyed reading this book, please leave a favorable review on Amazon.com

www.sandboxpersonalities.com

www.ingramcontent.com/pod-product-compliance
Lightning Source LLC
LaVergne TN
LVHW051607070426
835507LV00021B/2819